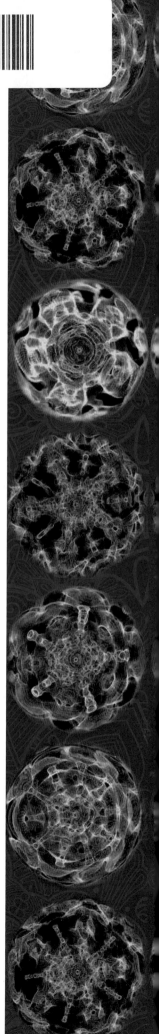

Soundflower by Mandara Cromwell

People Are Talking About *Soundflower*!

John Beaulieu, N.D., Ph.D.:

"I am always interested in the stories of Midwesterners who have discovered the 'eye of the tornado.' Mandara is the essence of Dorothy, who after being pulled into the eye of the tornado, discovers the mystical land of Oz and says to her dog, 'Toto, I have a feeling we are not in Kansas anymore.' Mandara begins her book *Soundflower* as a child playing in the farmlands of Kansas, where she has an alchemical dream, in which her limbs are separated from her body. In alchemical literature, this represents her transcending of the elements, allowing her to experience a spiritual transformation, during which her consciousness is liberated from the pull of the four elements (Air, Fire, Water, and Earth). She is now in the eye of the storm and being transported into mystical realms. …She floats in a golden hue, and she is transformed into thousands of diamonds as she is guided to sound healing.

"Sound Healing is a universal field of knowledge that is not bound by profession. Everyone integrates sound into their lives in thousands of different ways. Mandara was guided to cymatics and psychoacoustic sound applications via a cymatics-application device developed by Peter Guy Manners. I first came into contact with Peter Guy Manners and his cymatic-application device in 1981 in Cambridge, Mass., during a Sound Healers Association meeting. Like Mandara, I was impressed with the idea of the device and not so much with Peter Guy Manners. At the time, I observed many treatments and also experienced a treatment myself. I did not witness any miracle healings, and in general, I was turned off by him. This amounted to a felt sense of distrust, based on secret frequencies, questionable credentials, and a lot of alcohol consumption.

"At the same time, I considered him a pioneer in sound healing. Being turned off by him didn't mean I dismissed him. I love *characters* and have spent many years working in psychiatric hospitals. So, quite the opposite. I liked Dr. Manners because my nature is always to look past character flaws and discover the 'baby in the bathwater.' Mandara's path took her into the essence of psychoacoustic cymatic applications via the cymatic device that Peter Guy Manners pioneered. She has, by her own story, brought the baby out of the bathwater with her new AMI 750 device, into the emerging field of sound healing. In doing so, she honors the memory of Peter Guy Manners as a pioneer in the sound healing field and brings his work to a new level."

Jeff Volk, poet, producer, and publisher:

"As one who has been deeply involved in both the physics of sound and vibration and the practice of therapeutic sound and music for three and a half decades, it is indeed refreshing for me to share my insights on *Soundflower*. The great accomplishment of cymatics is that it makes the invisible force of sound vibrations visible! Mandara's true-life story illustrates this so vividly, almost mythically, as she follows her dream to winnow out the essence of a therapeutic sound modality that is just now being realized.

"I have consistently been impressed with her creativity and commitment, her passion and perpetual perseverance. So it is with particular delight, that through this heartfelt *blossoming* of a *Soundflower*, I finally get to see so many seemingly disparate pieces come together in a coherent storyline—much like watching a delicate sound pattern emerge in front of my eyes. This is much more than a suspenseful memoir, it is a spiritual saga…one that outlines the sojourn of a woman who feels a calling and repeatedly summons up the courage to keep pursuing her goal as it shifts and changes in front of her eyes. Unfailing in her devotion, unflinching in her discipline and dedication, I have great confidence that she will indeed fulfill her destiny."

Catherine Tanner, M.D., Electrons RX US:

"Mandara Cromwell is one of the most integrous, compassionate and passionate healers I have ever met. She has the most amazing ability to integrate seamlessly intuition with the science that is the most prevalent method of healing in the west. Her melding of sound therapy, Chinese medicine and the current state of knowledge of the human body is the perfect vehicle for the future of true healing. I can attest to the efficacy of the AMI 750 both personally and professionally."

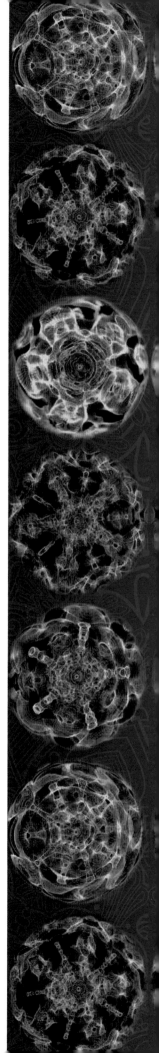

Thomas Antone, Doctor of Chiropractic:

"It is oft repeated that some of the greatest scientific discoveries are equal parts hard work and serendipity. Mandara takes you on a journey—sometimes intrepid, sometimes serene—that led her to develop what may be the harbinger of 'frequency medicine' for the world. You will be delighted as you learn of the mysterious origins and development of the world's first AMI (Acoustic Meridian Intelligence) device. Her candor and honest personal assessments are as refreshing as they are moving. A gem!"

Robert J. Gilbert, Ph.D., Director of the Vesica Institute for Holistic Studies:

"Cymatics has the ability to make invisible vibrations visibly appear, demonstrating the reality behind all ancient and modern vibrational healing sciences. Mandara Cromwell is at the forefront of creating new technology, which applies these cymatic vibrations therapeutically. This long-awaited book from Mandara will make her important contributions known to a much wider audience, whose lives can greatly benefit from these healing breakthroughs."

James Oliverio, Director and Professor Digital Worlds Institute, University of Florida:

"Ms. Cromwell's ongoing journey of discovery is a fascinating and inspiring reminder of the healing power of acoustic energy. *Soundflower* is both a poignant portrait of a modern innovator and a call to regain our consciousness of the primordial."

Graphic and Interior Design: Mandara Cromwell
                          Kate Holland

Design Consultants: Stephen Walker
                    Debby Lusk

CymaGlyphs: John Stuart Reid

Editor: Stephen J. Miller

Proof Reader: Heather Holley

ISBN-13: 978-0-9993100-0-7

Library of Congress: 2018912067

1. Health and Wellness—Sound Healing. 2. Memoir—New Thought, Entrepreneurship. 3. Inspiration and Personal Growth—Sound Meditation. 4. Art—Cymatics, Sound-Made-Visible Images. I. Title

Mandara Cromwell has written *Soundflower* as a guide for spiritual advancement. The techniques and the devices discussed here are not a replacement for medical care or advice. Her products and programs come with specific instructions, which must be adhered to for the full utilization of the therapy. Her company and employees abide by the regulations of the FDA in the use of the products and in the creation of the educational materials.

Printed By:

Taylor Specialty Books
Dallas, Texas
United States of America

If you would like to contact the author or view other products, please visit:
www.cymatechnologies.com

SOUNDFLOWER

The Journey To Marry Science and Spirit

MANDARA CROMWELL

Table of Contents

DEDICATION

To My Beloved~

To All My Beloveds Who Have Met Me Along The Path

I am grateful to you for holding the mirror so that I may see my own reflection as I seek Truth and Love

To my beloved father who encouraged me to listen for the voices of the angels

To my beloved mother who taught me strength and courage—a girl can do whatever she sets her mind to

To my beloved grandmother who loved me unconditionally and taught me to pray: to ask God, "Why?"and be willing to hear the answer

To my beloved daughter who is the earthly representation of a divine mother

To my beloved sisters, each of whom I honor for choosing their own precious paths

To my beloved spiritual teachers who taught me discipline and the hidden knowledge of the spiritual world

To my beloved, who is an inspiration in philosophy, art, and science

To my beloved, who taught me to be gentle and compassionate with everyone

To my beloved, who when I asked for business advice replied, "No one knows the answer to your question, because no one has done this before. You will find your way."

To my beloved, who stood by me with compassion as I crumbled into dust and then watched as I rose from the ashes

To my beloved, who patiently waits as I dance around the garland of life to find the garden entrance

To my beloved, who keeps my feet on the path, holds me when I weep, and joins me in celebration

To all of my Beloveds, You know who you are

I love you with all my heart and dedicate this book to you.

FOREWARD

By

John Stuart Reid

Of all the books ever written, only a handful have held the power to change the world. In the realm of science, Robert Hooke's *Micrographia*, Isaac Newton's *Principia Mathmatica,* and Charles Darwin's *The Origin of Species* are three of very few that can be said to have radically shifted our beliefs and provided lasting benefits for humanity. I believe that the book you now hold in your hands carries the potential for great change in the realm of physical well-being.

The mainstream modality of therapeutic ultrasound—high frequency (inaudible) sound—can support the body to recover from soft tissue injury and severe bone fractures. What is less well known is that audible sound can also support the body to heal physical trauma as well as provide lasting relief from chronic pain and other health challenges. These important health-giving gifts for humanity were espoused by Pythagoras of Samos 2,500 years ago. He believed that music held the keys to physical well-being. History reports that Pythagoras traveled extensively in ancient Egypt, and it seems possible that he learned this therapeutic concept from the priesthood-healers.

Fast forward to 1997 when I, too, was traveling to Egypt to conduct a series of acoustics experiments in the Great Pyramid. I had severely injured my lower back three weeks before flying to Cairo, and I was in agonizing pain as I set up the acoustic test equipment; yet, within twenty minutes of switching on the sound source, all the pain left my body. At the end of the three hours' research session I felt so strong and pain free that I was able to assist in carrying the heavy cases. The pain never returned. The experiments proved to be a great success and shed light on the acoustics aspect of the King's Chamber design. Yet the question that remained with me in the years that followed was this: what is the sonic mechanism that has the power to cause severe pain to miraculously vanish?

Soundflower is the journey of a woman who was called to bring a unique type of sound therapy to the world, a modality that has no known side effects and offers an abundance of health-giving benefits for both humans and animals. Mandara Cromwell has dedicated her life, indefatigably, to creating a system based on audible sound to free people from chronic pain as well as a myriad of health challenges. She is a woman of clear vision and deep passion who has created a natural, noninvasive technique to support the body's ability to heal itself through specific sound frequencies.

I hold deep respect and appreciation for the positive difference her work is making in people's lives. I need no convincing that sound holds the power to create form from formlessness; in my daily work as an acoustics-physics researcher I remain fascinated by the beauty of sound's vibrations imprinted on pure water, revealing its hidden geometries. And I need no convincing that sound has transformative powers for physiology: I became a believer in twenty minutes, twenty years ago in the Great Pyramid of Egypt. I have spent many years exploring the mechanisms that underpin sound therapy, and I now share my findings and insights into sound's restorative powers at conferences worldwide. In using Ms. Cromwell's sound therapy device, my family and I have witnessed time and again its efficacy.

In reading Mandara Cromwell's story, I have no doubt that you too will come to believe in the transformative power of sound.

John Stuart Reid, Acoustics Physics Researcher, United Kingdom 2017

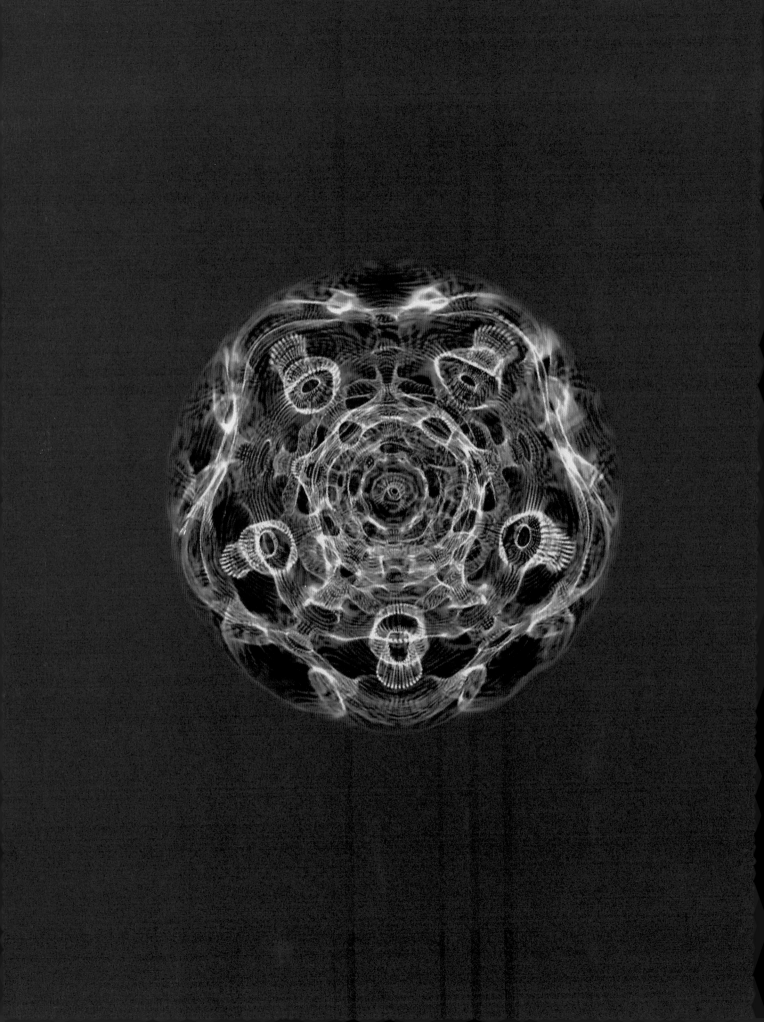

PREFACE

If you are fascinated by the images on the cover and the side panels of the introductory pages, you are one of many who are becoming interested in a the relatively new discovery: of *cymatics*, which is the science of making sound visible. The *sound flowers* that are the illustrations throughout this book are pure sound images, not digitally created. Through the invention of the *CymaScope,* by acoustics physics researcher John Stuart Reid, we can see sound made visible. The frequency patterns were created from sound generated by the AMI (Acoustic Meridian Intelligence) series of devices, which I invented.

Many people are seeking answers while on their spiritual journey toward a more natural way of healing body, mind, and spirit. This book is an intimate look at the many revelations I experienced on my own path while learning about sound—and the healing potential of the images sound can produce.

Soundflower is my first book. It has taken me almost a lifetime to write. It has been my mission to prove with science what I first knew to be true in my own heart. Many life-learning experiences, coupled with new scientific discoveries in the field of *sound science,* have finally confirmed what I somehow already knew. Found in this book are glimpses of the profoundly beautiful universe, which can help us all.

As you read this book, I ask you to do so with an open mind and heart. If it can accomplish one thing, my hope is that it will inspire you to embark on your own spiritual journey with great faith, knowing that the keys to your destiny can truly be found.

There are signs and symbols everywhere that lead us home.

Mandara Cromwell
Atlanta, Georgia, 2018

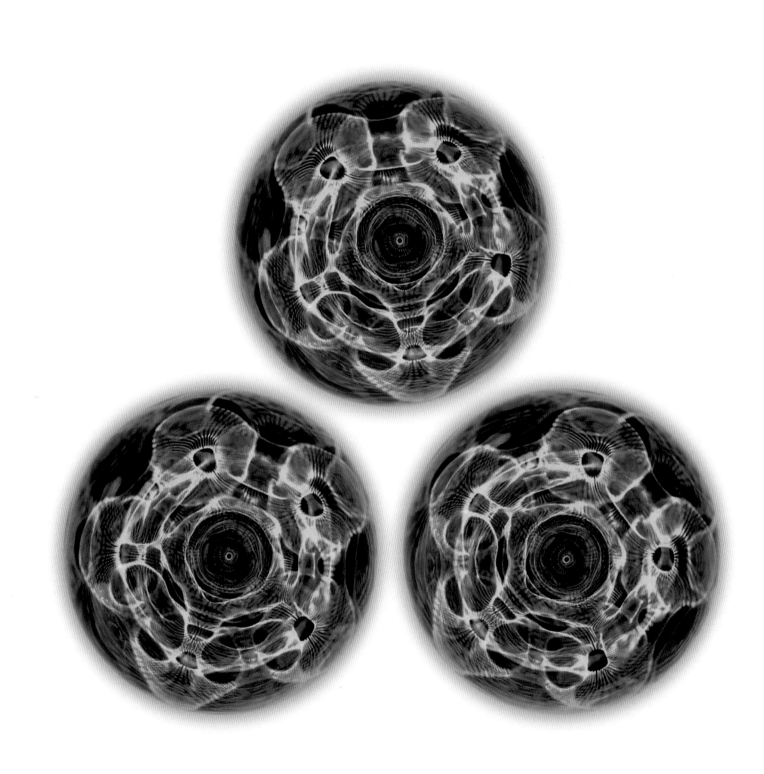

INTRODUCTION
Entering the World of Cymatics

The very simple definition of "cymatics" is the science of making sound visible. It was developed during recent decades through the work of Hans Jenny, a Swiss medical doctor and natural scientist. During the late 1940s, Dr. Peter Guy Manners, whose work I continue to evolve, was researching the *biosignatures* of the body. As a tribute to the work of Dr. Jenny, he named his technique *cymatic therapy*. In 2002, when I rebirthed this therapy with the new device I had innovated, I decided to call it simply *Cymatherapy*.

Currently, many people are looking at cymatic images on the internet. A classic example shows many mysterious and beautiful geometric shapes, created by the vibrations of a violin bow stroking a metal plate sprinkled with sand. Some of these early experiments, and other images you see online today, were made with only one frequency.

When I first viewed the video of Dr. Jenny's experiment using multiple frequencies and metal filings, I was astounded: the particles stood up off the plate and expressed themselves in three dimensions. I watched them glide across a membrane in an amazing response to the sound. This was one of my early experiences of seeing the ability of sound to create form (years before, I had studied yantras, an integral part of Vedic studies and an ancient form of mantras made visible).

The more I studied cymatic images, the more I became aware that these symbols have appeared in art and architecture for thousands of years. (Each time I witness some form of these sacred images, I feel mystical truths are being revealed to me.) It has been written throughout the centuries that some architects and builders encoded their structures with ancient knowledge through a sort of hieroglyphic language, which in many ways resembles cymatic imagery. It appears they created symbols to hold information, sometimes from spiritual traditions and other times from specific schools of mystical thought.

For instance, on several occasions I have visited the Roslyn Chapel in Scotland where architectural cubes in the ceiling appear to be almost exact replicas of the early work of Ernst Chaldni (known as the "Father of Acoustics"), who made sound visible with metal plates and a violin bow back in the 1700s. In the chapel, the cubes—with sound-made-visible images—are attached to the arches in the ceiling in a musically sequential way. Confirming this, at the end of each row there is an angel playing music, each one with a different kind of instrument.

When the sound represented on these cubes is played by classical musicians, it produces a hauntingly beautiful melody. This was discovered after much research by composers Thomas and Stuart Mitchell. They decoded the sacred geometrical patterns and musical intonations of each of the cubes. Their composition can be found online by searching for "the Roslyn Motet."

While I enjoy looking at artistic cymatic images, generally they are made from just one frequency or are digitally created. My most powerful experiences consist of viewing cymatic glyphs that were produced by the CymaScope, using codes with five frequencies, for healing and regeneration. I believe when an image is generated by a healing sound, it brings about a state of divine awareness.

The cymatic images I am working with now are created in a controlled laboratory setting with great technical expertise. The five frequencies generated by the AMI 750 device are expressed in a multi-dimensional visual image, allowing the viewer to experience sound coming to life. I can only describe these *sound flowers* as spiritual doorways. When gazing into them, they can become a gateway to meditation.

Viewing one of the images is like plunging into a sea of sound: while watching, it is easy to become a part of it. The energy of the cymatic glyph will expand and surround you. I am in awe of how complex and beautiful it is. Each one has a depth that allows you to be transported into a higher state of yourself. It is very comforting, because it's something you recognize within your innate knowing. Through the sound flowers, you can come into the realization of your own form in its fullness.

PHOTO BY JOHN STUART REID, ROSSLYN CHAPEL, SCOTLAND

Please join me in exploring the beauty of the cymatic universe.

Soundflower

THE JOURNEY TO MARRY SCIENCE AND SPIRIT

MANDARA CROMWELL

"I invite you to gaze into the heart

of the sound flowers…"

—Mandara

PROLOGUE

From the time I was little, I found nature to be mystical and magical. Playing outside in the farmlands of Kansas, I was filled with the joy of discovering endless treasures: the sound of the cottonwood leaves rustling in the wind, the trickling of nearby streams, and the giant lilac bush that bloomed beautifully every year without fail. I was entranced by the purpling of the night sky, filled with a thousand stars. I never tired of the majesty of the universe. That was how I perceived science.

There exists what most people consider to be science, and then there is the phrase: "new science." I smile when I hear it, because new science often debunks what old science was sure of. My true interest in science concerns one of the most powerful forces in the universe—sound. Now, with the relatively new science of cymatics, we can see it made visible.

When I make presentations about cymatics or Cymatherapy, many people are skeptical. They listen to these ideas with minds full of doubt. However, in my search for knowledge, I have found in ancient texts and teachings the basis of conclusions that I like to call "new sound science." As I work toward my goal of bringing more understanding to the idea of sound as a healing modality, I have to point out that we have been using various applications of it for decades. The ultrasound devices used in doctors' offices today are the most obvious example (though most everyone admits science still can't explain exactly how ultrasound works).

The more scientists can see with high powered microscopes and diagnostic devices, the more they are discovering the interesting and miraculous ways cells communicate. Sound remains one of the most profound ways we can affect matter. As I watch this new science develop, I am reminded of great inventors and intellectuals who have found ways to construct buildings and create new inventions by studying and even imitating the dynamic symmetrical patterns found in nature. These motifs are repeated over and over again for us to enjoy and learn from.

For me, the patterns of the ancient yantras are the greatest examples of drawing science and spirit together through the sacred geometry created by sound. The images show us how intricate geometric structures can be ensouled by sound. The spiritual adepts who chanted the ancient mantras could actually see the energetic patterns their words created. They used the geometric shapes to record what they repeatedly witnessed in energetic forms.

This knowledge has been handed down through the generations and sometimes kept hidden in order to protect it. I believe this is also true with the healing power of sound. As my search for proof of this power has intensified, I have been inspired to investigate further how cells communicate. Because of this, I happened upon *biotensegrity*, which reveals the most sacred inner structure of the cell whereupon sound travels and moves through. *Tensegrity*, it turns out, is an architectural term that describes a unique way to balance weight in giant buildings and a means to handle the stresses placed on large structures like skyscrapers. Tensegrity, as it applies to the human body, is a protective mechanism. With the way sound travels through these structures, I envision it helps to balance the stresses within cells as well.

The universe is filled with great forces and incredible gifts created for us. Sound is one of those forces, whose potential we are just beginning to realize. I hope my story will inspire people to look deeper into the places where science and spirit connect. The signs are everywhere.

Chapter One

The Initiation

I believe that each person will come to recognize a moment when the true journey of their life begins. My own quest started when I was just a little girl....

Growing up in a small town in Kansas, I lived in a very close knit community with my parents who were farmers. We had chickens, cows, and a horse named Blue Moon that my father took me for many joy-filled rides on. Gravel roads connected us to the nearest town of about 900 people, which was easily a twenty-minute drive each way by car. We made this trip weekly on most Sundays.

I remember at age five attending St. Gregory's Catholic Church. It was built in a traditional Gothic style, which I found exciting—with its gilded buttresses and painted angels on the ceiling. There were mysterious nooks, colorful stained glass windows, and towering archways pointing to the sky. This immense beauty led to many grand imaginings. Especially as a child growing up in the farmlands of Kansas, where there were few examples of architectural splendor on such a grand scale.

One of my fondest memories of being at that church was tugging at my father's suit jacket and exclaiming as I gazed at the massive ceiling, "Look at the angels! Look at the angels!"

"Shhh!" he said, with his fingers to his lips. He bent down and whispered in my ear, "If you're not quiet, you won't be able to hear what they are saying."

There it was—my first instruction on how to listen for the voices of the angels! It came from my father. He introduced me to the idea there could be spiritual messengers, and from that point forward, I was always listening. I believed they wanted to talk to me. Gazing at the angels on the ceiling during the church service, I became fascinated with the glowing circles around their heads, which I first perceived as their "golden hats."

As I stared intently, their halos pulsed with tiny particles like the finest starlight. The music of the choir filtered through the air and the halos became brighter. I felt the sound within me while the angelic beings hovered above. This experience gave me my first visual of how sound could make things resonate.

During my years in grammar school, I would become secretly excited when the nuns came to the classroom to announce that someone had passed away. This meant we would be asked to sing the Latin Requiem for the departed soul and permitted to go into what was the normally forbidden choir loft, allowing us to be close to the colossal pipe organ and the painted angels on the ceiling.

As we sang, I looked over the balcony and watched the funeral in progress. I could literally *see* the energy that was manifesting: sometimes in swirling discs, sometimes as stars, and all of it in many different colors. There were silken strands of light coming from the angels above, who had opened doorways into the expansive universe. I could see the soul of the departed being raised up! Being close to the powerful undercurrent of the pipe organ gave me a sense the whole choir was being propelled into an energetic and mysterious flight.

There was a favorite vocalist for these rites who sang "Ave Maria." Her voice was brilliant and pure, filling the Gothic architecture. In my heart, I felt it filling me, too. As the vibrations of the music became stronger and the octaves rose higher, I could feel the sound beneath my skin. The pipe organ kindled the atmosphere—sparking the walls into a pulsating new experience.

The music lifted my soul while the particles of the *golden hats* accelerated their twinkling. Many gleaming-yellow layers of energy appeared in the rising incense. All around me, close to my body, there was a sense of brightness. I felt as though I were being raised into the air and was sure I could take flight! This was my first awareness of how sound could lift me up. Memories of my first church are replete with these experiences.

My parents, who were devout Catholics, received an extensive collection of books that had belonged to my grandparents. In turn, these were lovingly passed down to me and cherished, in part, because we had a very few books in our home library. From age ten through thirteen, I became fully immersed in the stories of St. Rose of Lima, St. Theresa of Avilla, St. Catherine of Sienna, and St. Francis of Assisi. My favorite was St. Therese of Lisieux, who was known as "the Little Flower." I read these stories over and over and imagined myself in each one of them. The sincere spiritual quests of the saints had a great impact on me; I spent hours contemplating what it was like to know God through their experiences.

These volumes and their lessons, the rituals of the Catholic church, and the visions of the saints with their offerings of spiritual guidance all seemed quite natural to me. When I read the stories in my early teens I would think, "If I could just be a flower in the garden of the Lord, that would be the goal for my life."

Later, when I was sixteen years old, I began to question things. I asked my parents if I had to continue going to church. I was having some serious doubts about what appeared to be more of a social gathering. In my own spiritual quest, I was looking for no less than the mystical teachings of Christ; I longed to have the experiences of the saints. My parents, however, insisted I continue to go, even if all the answers weren't immediately available to me.

Unfortunately, the original church I attended was torn down and its magnificence lost. It makes me sad to think about it. I loved the beauty of that church and my early experiences there. Now, when I currently struggle with an issue, I will still go visit a holy place, sit quietly, and remember the spiritual experiences I have had in my life. There are countless paths with many teachers, and I have searched for truth in a lot of places.

I attended Washburn University (a small liberal arts college in Topeka, Kansas), without ascribing to any specific course of study. I saw college as a time of investigation. One of the classes that appealed to me most was philosophy—especially Eastern philosophy. When I read about reincarnation, the rebirth of the soul into a new body, it made perfect sense to me; I was very accepting of the possibility. I discovered this concept during a time when eastern Indian culture was becoming of interest in our society.

It was the late '60s, a time in history when young people were experimenting with drugs while others were vision seeking, or some combination of the two. Seeing this happen around me, I realized I wanted the spiritual fulfillment others were achieving. I saw them utilizing gurus, teachers who could take one from spiritual darkness to light. I wondered what it would be like to learn from such a master.

While attending a class in astronomy, my curiosity about the stars led me to astrology and other esoteric teachings. Some of the books by Alice Bailey, a Theosophist and popular writer of New Age subjects, were especially profound. She wrote about achieving higher states of consciousness without having to use drugs, a path I was definitely attracted to. My years in college were not party years. Unlike the new friends I had made, I preferred to stay in my room and immerse myself in various spiritual discourses (even now, I still consider myself to be somewhat of an introvert).

At the end of four years of study, I still wasn't sure of my direction. With an art history degree, there was really only one thing to do, teach. But at that time, a teaching career held no interest for me. However, there was no escaping the fact I needed a job.

I moved to Scottsdale, Arizona (being somewhat familiar with it as my grandparents had spent their winters there), and I learned of a position as a fashion model in a downtown restaurant during afternoon tea. Monday through Friday, it was the practice of some local department stores to showcase their latest upscale, sophisticated clothing at this boutique restaurant.

Several other models worked with me, and the clothes were certainly fashionable, but they weren't my style; they were for a much older crowd. I do remember a day when a fancy, multi-colored silk caftan was provided for me to model. It was probably the closest to my taste back then; surprisingly, it was also popular with the ladies who were purchasing garments.

My mother had a saying, though: "The day is long if you aren't doing something you love." In my heart, I knew there was something else I was supposed to be doing. There was somewhere else I longed to be. I continued my studies in various new age philosophies such as astrology, self development techniques (like EST), herbal medicine (I studied personally with Dr. John Christopher), and my search for truth persisted with a host of teachers. I worked during the week and met a boyfriend who was interested in a similar spiritual path.

In 1974, we planned to take a trip to Colorado. While in Aspen, we visited an EST center which offered specialized training for personal development, created by Werner Erhard. We had both taken these kinds of workshops previously. My boyfriend decided to stay in Aspen, while I headed home to Kansas for a short visit with my parents. It was during that side trip I experienced the most profound dream of my whole life.

One night, after an enjoyable dinner with my parents, I retired to a bedroom on the second floor of our farmhouse. This was the room my younger sister and I had shared during our growing up years. Our home was nestled between several of my family's farming fields, near a river. Just knowing the water was there provided me with a deep sense of peace. I quickly fell asleep, and the dream started to unfold.

It began with me walking down a path where everything was like a black and white photograph, layered with misty shades of gray. In the distance, I could see three figures coming toward me, all dressed in white. I noticed that my shoe was untied, and I crouched down to fix it. In my peripheral vision, I could see the three strangers very close now and deep in conversation. I couldn't hear what they were saying, but I thought it best not to stand up and risk interrupting them. I assumed they would walk around me.

Then, coming toward me, the one in the middle pulled out a large sword crafted in both gold and silver, encrusted with jewels. This figure was androgynous, with male and female qualities balanced perfectly, full of refinement and beauty. The other two beings moved in slowly and gracefully, pausing on either side of me. They pulled out daggers that were smaller versions of the larger more dazzling sword. The central figure used the sword to pierce my spine. The other two used their daggers to slice across my shoulders. Despite the shocking nature of this, at no time did I experience any pain, blood, or suffering.

At that moment, I drifted into another vignette. Softly changing, the black and white of the images transformed into a brilliant Technicolor. Strangely, I found myself in a morgue, lying on a table with a white sheet covering me up to my neck. Everything around me shimmered with a golden hue.

When I looked to my right, there was a table next to me. On it was a man with dark brown skin, dressed in a loin cloth. He was lying on his side with his head propped up in his hand. At first glimpse, I thought he was wearing a rosary, but later learned to recognize this necklace as *mala* beads, a sacred tool for meditation. The individual beads were highly unusual. They were round, reddish brown, and for some reason, I couldn't take my eyes off of them. Afterward, I learned they were *rudrakshas*, which are highly prized, valuable seeds associated with Lord Shiva. There was a long string of them draped across his chest.

When our eyes met, he said, "Well! You know you're immortal now."

To try to make logical sense of what was happening, I diverted my attention by gazing at the ceiling. Above me, another stunning vision came into view. I could see myself standing on the precipice of a cliff. Bravely, I took a step into the dark sky. In a flash of light, I became formless, filled with thousands of iridescent diamonds. I was aware of every shimmering particle and became one with the experience.

When I woke up the next morning, I stayed in bed for a long time contemplating the meaning of the mystical vision. It stayed with me for days and days. Even now, I can still see it all clearly—relive each moment easily. In the years that followed, in my practice of Siddha yoga, I became convinced that the dream signified an initiation, and I had become *spiritually activated*. It will certainly have a stunning effect on me forever.

Later that day, when I went for a ride with my Dad, I was trying to explain my dream to him. I told him I had become immortal. He gave me a look with a little bit of a smile that said, "Yes, that's my girl. Her ball bounces a little differently."

After visiting my parents, I rejoined my boyfriend back in Aspen. He had learned that the EST Center was sponsoring a tour of the Indian guru Swami Muktananda, founder of Siddha yoga. At the end of July 1974, there was a five-day meditation retreat, to be held outside of Denver. We drove there, and not knowing what to expect, I arrived in a fashionable miniskirt, high-heeled clogs, Jackie O. sunglasses, and a floppy hat. I was dressed for a celebratory weekend out of town; I had no idea what a life changing event this was to be.

We arrived at a campground and were guided to our lodgings in a rustic-style cabin with wooden floors and bunk beds. We gathered at another similar structure for dinner and were served a delicious vegetarian meal. I was seated across from an American woman, dressed in a sapphire blue sari, with eyes that shone with an inner light. She spoke very excitedly about the benefits of meditation, which I had only read about. Her presence alone inspired me to learn more about it. Little did I know, three years later, she would become my sister-in-law.

We were asked to wake up at 5:00 a.m. the next morning to meditate. As we walked into the hall, men and women were separated and directed to sit on opposite sides of the room. There were maybe twenty people sitting on the floor. Since I hadn't received instruction in the techniques the others were utilizing, I stayed near the back of the room. I sat down, closed my eyes, and started to relax. Periodically, I could hear more people entering the room to join the session.

Even though my eyes were closed, I sensed others getting up and down off the floor. This was accompanied by rhythmic breathing. I wanted to open my eyes, but I was already being pulled deeper into my own experience. I would come to learn that some of the sounds were of people practicing *kriyas* (vigorous yoga techniques), and the controlled breathing was called *pranayama*. In the moment, I did not know any of this though, and I soon fell into my own deep state of meditation. It was automatic; no effort on my part was needed.

At least an hour later, when I opened my eyes, I noticed someone sitting on a chair in the front of the room. It was Swami Muktananda; however, I recognized him as the man from my dream who spoke of my being immortal. I was stunned. I could barely believe my eyes. After a few minutes, when the meditation was over, he got up and left. I didn't tell anyone about my previous dream and the appearance of Swami Muktananda therein. I chose to keep this powerful realization to myself.

At one point during the retreat when I was outside walking alone, I saw Swami Muktananda in the distance. Baba, as he was known, was smiling and walking toward me with another gentleman, who was his translator. When he got within talking distance, he spoke to me through him and said, "How does it feel now that you are immortal?"

Baba didn't stop to hear my reply but continued walking by.

"Wait a minute! What did he just say?" I thought to myself, as I watched him walk away. I wondered how he could have tuned in to my dream.

As the retreat studies progressed, I began to learn Sanskrit chanting. It is known as the language of vibration, which I wasn't surprised to discover. While chanting, I recognized the resonance generated as the same energy I experienced when I heard "Ava Maria" in church as a child. Back then, I felt the sound lifting me up; here, the Sanskrit aided in focusing the sound on clearing my *mental body*. It created a beautiful buzzing in the crown of my head.

I recognized chanting as a tool to build *shakti*, a mystical energy which could be awakened by using particular Sanskrit syllables. The upward moving vibrations began at the base of my spine and traveled into every crevice in my torso and limbs. A certain type of inner heat streamed upward, clearing the energetic pathways as it climbed to the top of my head.

Each of the Sanskrit sounds had an effect in my oral cavity. As my tongue tapped at the roof of my mouth, it produced an experience that was both intoxicating and full of spiritual ecstasy. I could see each syllable form a colorful, vibratory pattern. Rippling outward, each one expanded to permeate the space around me. I was elated but mystified. How was this happening? I would come to understand that my tongue taps, part of the spiritual practice of chanting the Sanskrit, stimulated the eighty-four reflex points in the mouth, thereby affecting the chemistry and neurotransmitters of the brain.

When the retreat came to completion, before I returned home to Scottsdale, I purchased a picture of Baba. During my studies that week, I had learned the technique of setting up a meditation area at home. It was important to create a personal place, to sit quietly, and continue to build my spiritual connection to Baba.

When I got home, I placed his picture on a small wooden table and created my new sacred space. Building this area reminded me of my early years of Catholicism, when I placed pictures and statues of Jesus, Mary, and the saints throughout our home. During my process now, Swami Muktananda was constantly in my thoughts, and as days went by, I kept thinking of ways I could get back to see him again. I spoke to his picture, telling him everything in my mind and heart.

"Baba, I feel I need to spend more time with you, to receive your direct instruction," I often repeated. "I would like an indefinite period of study with you, but I haven't enough money for a lengthy stay."

A short time afterward, I started having problems with my furnace; although, it appeared to be nothing serious. A repairman had already been called by the landlord to come and check it. However, a few days later while I was at work, I received a phone call telling me there had been an explosion. My house had burned to the ground. I was devastated. I realized I had no clothes, no belongings—not even a toothbrush. How could this have happened to me? Why should I have to go through this? It took the next six weeks to pull myself together.

While I was waiting to collect the insurance money, I had a realization. In a certain way, the fire was a financial gift, which could allow me to go on the spiritual journey my heart desired. I knew Swami Muktananda was still touring the United States, and this was my chance to request time to study with him.

Though many people went to learn meditation from Baba through retreats and weekend intensives, these were limited times of study in his physical presence. Asking to join the tour and live in the ashram was a much bigger commitment. It would be far more in depth, say, than taking a few classes at the local college. It was a total life change.

I saw that his tour took him close by, just outside of Albuquerque. Now was the time. All the signs were pointing toward it, so I decided to give in fully. It took a lot of courage to make the decision to go, but I was now intent upon having the full experience.

I hadn't had any communication with him or his staff since my last participation, so when I arrived at the retreat site I wanted to speak with him immediately, to let him know my true intentions. I wanted him to know how serious I was about pursuing this spiritual quest. Surprisingly, as I got out of the car, he was the first person I saw. He was a short distance away, walking again with his translator. Suddenly, I became fearful and full of doubt. The visions I had seen and all that I had personally experienced with him were rushing through my head. What if I had imagined it all?

I could see Baba speaking words to his translator. Then, he motioned me over. I walked toward him in amazement. Had he been waiting for me? I was overcome with the sense that this meeting was somehow predestined.

The translator spoke these words: "How are you doing since your house burned down?"

I was stunned, unable to answer.

In that moment, I became fully aware of how connected he was to what was happening in my life. I recognized his omniscient powers and knew I would have a new home with him, wherever he was. It felt as if I were being reshaped into fine silk, as though I were part of a new field of influence that was shifting every nanosecond into a higher consciousness. Nothing I had ever known compared to this shakti.

We stood on a grassy hill at the edge of a pathway we had walked to. With the late afternoon sun glowing all around us, I expressed my sincere wish to study with him and be in his presence.

"When can you come?" he asked.

It was decided I would meet him one month later in Oakland, California, to join his American tour. I was elated, excited, and so very grateful. It was my next chapter, my new beginning.

I would be allowed to live in his recently renovated ashram, which had been an old hotel, once inhabited by drug dealers and homeless people. In May of 1975, when I arrived, I only brought modest clothing and a very few personal items. I already knew that nothing more would be required for life at the ashram. Baba's women devotees generally wore long skirts, to allow for sitting on the floor during meditation. I didn't own any saris, which are the customary clothes for Indian women to wear, but I had been told this was not a requirement for living at the ashram.

After getting settled, I had my first *darshan* with Baba. In this first meeting he said, "You will be the flower girl." This meant I was to collect all the flowers that people brought as gifts to the guru and place them around the ashram. Shortly after this, however, Baba became ill. We were unable to receive flowers from the guests and devotees anymore, as the doctors believed he had become allergic to them. I was moved from my position as flower girl to registration.

At first, this was a disappointment. I had become accustomed to seeing him each morning from my work place in the small garden shed, where I prepared the flowers to put in vases. It was adjacent to the courtyard—a private space—where Baba would meet with the devotees. No one was allowed there, except during times of darshan with him. I enjoyed the days when he would throw pieces of candy to us from his second floor balcony, overlooking the courtyard. These sweets were considered highly treasured gifts from the guru, called *prasad*.

Although at first disheartened about my move to the registration desk, my disappointment soon vanished. I was able to see Baba on his morning stroll, in much closer proximity, as he passed by my desk. Looking into his eyes, I was transported to an indescribable place. It was a precious gift to meet him on a soul level each day. My heart was filled with devotion.

On my birthday, I had a special darshan with him. With great anticipation, I asked, "Baba, do I have a spiritual name?" (A spiritual name is something you had to request. Not everyone got one.)

"Yes," he replied. "You are Mandara."

When I asked the translator what it meant, he told me: "Flower."

The name "Mandara" refers to one of four heavenly flowers mentioned in the Vedas. I was thrilled and humbled to receive it. I meditated on it, to consider what his reasons for giving it to me could be. I connected it to the wish I had as a young girl in the Catholic church: to become a "flower of the Lord."

I adopted the name Mandara with my whole heart. It has been my authentic name since I received it. It was fitting to be given that name by Baba because, in retrospect, I can see that he was my spiritual father. The guru-disciple relationship had been established much longer than I consciously knew, and the more awakened I became, the more I understood who he was and the influence his teachings had upon me. He touched thousands of lives during my time at the ashram, and he initiated many into the next chapter of their spiritual journey.

Late in 1975, Baba announced to the devotees in the ashram that we would all be boarding a jumbo jet and going to India. He also extended the invitation to anyone else who wanted to go. He explained that everyone would be going to live in his ashram in Ganeshpuri. I had no fear about going. I only knew I wanted to be near my teacher, wherever he wanted us to be.

I will never forget the day we landed in Bombay. The whole plane ride had felt celebratory, as if we were traveling to a new dimension on an incredible journey. But, when the door of the plane opened, I was aghast. The whole plane became permeated with a horrible smell. India's system for disposing waste was still very primitive, and I felt myself gagging, struggling desperately not to throw up. This was not a Hollywood movie; this was my new life — with all the thrills and challenges that one must face in a new world.

We exited the plane with scarves over our faces. There was no security check back then, so we quickly boarded buses that took us on a two-hour ride over dusty dirt roads to Ganeshpuri. It was at the end of the monsoon season, so the level of humidity was something I had never experienced before. When we arrived at the ashram, we were pleasantly surprised to find new dormitories had been built adjacent to it. I was thrilled to be in India, amidst the growing number of devotees coming to live with Baba, to pursue what I believed to be a truly spiritual life.

In the weeks that followed, I experienced incredible heights of meditative joy while being allowed to be an attendant of the Shiva temple, where the Lord of Yoga is honored. It was part of my work to help maintain this small building on the ashram property so that other devotees could come and visit there.

A wall was built around the ashram, and with its extensive acreage, it served as a sacred space for spiritual practices and for the protection of the devotees and animals who lived there. Not to mention the literally hundreds of people who were coming to see Baba, from nearby and around the world, on a daily basis. The weekends were particularly busy. He would often go into seclusion, to rest himself, in order to maintain the level of energy it took to be in the presence of so many followers. His living quarters, located in the central part of the ashram complex, were adjacent to the main temple.

Baba designed the whole property to facilitate the journey of the aspirant. There was an indescribable beauty throughout. Many of the memories I hold dear are of days in the upper garden, where the Shiva Temple was located. My meditative walks on the way there took me on a path through rice paddies to an area where many statues of Indian saints and sages stood. Most of them had been sculpted by devotees who had lived at the ashram and were inspired to express their creativity as part of their service.

Baba would often bring the wisdom or teachings of these saints into the discourses he shared with us. There were places designated along the pathway to sit near the statues during times of contemplation. They evoked a great sense of peace in me. Roses were planted all along the way, with many other bushes and natural grasses. This eventually led to the main rose garden, full of rows of bushes that required a lot of attention due to the constant heat.

Nearby was the *yagna mandap*, an outdoor pavilion in the upper garden used by Brahmin priests for sacred rituals. It was a huge slab of concrete with a vented metal roof (to allow smoke to leave during fire ceremonies). Thousands of people could congregate underneath it, at the request of Baba, during special rituals performed by the priests.

The fire ceremony was held several times each year as part of a spiritual purification. These occasions were filled with the constant repetition of Sanskrit prayers, in their specific poetic meter, commanding attention and deep reverence from all in the area.

During these times, I had some of my most profound visions. As I walked the pathway nearby, it would feel as if the air had been rarified. The atmosphere was filled with luminous spheres of various shades of blue—a myriad of jewel-like particles. This was a vision I saw with my eyes open, unlike the ones I had experienced during meditation. The air was so charged with these particles, that it gave me another dimension of physical sight. An invisible world was shown to me. Walking amidst this space was an opportunity to be cleansed by pure sound.

In the upper garden, where the Shiva temple was located, a lotus pool had been created. It held some thirty to forty plants, which bloomed seasonally, in a large circular metal tank with a ledge for seating. This was adjacent to the shed that was home for Baba's elephant, Vijay. Nearby was the barn for sacred cows. Devotees who provided loving care for the grounds also brought water for the animals as part of their daily service.

Baba had a very special relationship with his elephant. His full name was Vijayananda, which meant "the Bliss of Victory (of reaching enlightenment)." Everyone knew him as Baba's elephant, or Vijay. During holiday celebrations, Vijay was adorned with Indian blankets and bells. His coverings were very colorful and helped to create a spectacle as he paraded through the grounds. The devotees drew sacred mandalas on him with colored chalk. Vijay was perfectly happy, until Baba would leave the ashram for any length of time. On those occasions, he would cry, make very loud noises, and run out of his area of the garden.

Vijay was unable to escape the compound, but had to be brought back to his barn by the devotees, which was no easy feat. He wasn't as tame as animals seen in the circus, so

Baba would be called and asked to hurry home. When he arrived, he spoke to Vijay in Hindi and shook a large stick in the air. He never touched the animal with the stick. The translator explained that Baba was telling the elephant his behavior was incorrect.

To calm him, Baba would anoint the area between his eyes with special sandalwood or khus oil. Vijay's anxiety would go away almost immediately. Then Baba would bring a chair and sit next to him. The two of them would rest in peaceful communion. Vijay was the ultimate disciple who just wanted to be near his teacher. He loved Baba with true devotion.

As I sat in the upper garden, on the cool marble stairs of the temple, I could view many powerful symbols, which I believed reflected the significant aspects of my spiritual life. To me, Vijay was the living representation of the great Hindu deity Ganesha, remover of obstacles. I had trust in the power of Ganesha to help dispel difficulties. I witnessed this kind of love when I saw Baba with Vijay. The lotus pool was filled with delicate white and pink flowers rising from the mud, symbolic of purity and spiritual rebirth. I saw how the devotees changed from the darkness of unconsciousness into the full bloom of self-realization. On the other side, Brahmin priests often filled the area with chanting and purifying fire. Once again, the sound of the sacred words were symbolic to me. All of these aspects joined in my heart, and I knew I was in the right place.

The biggest challenge at this point in my journey was the oppressive heat that came at the end of the monsoon season. I would start my meditation practice at 3 a.m. before the temperature escalated, which happened quickly even in the early morning hours. With a flashlight, I walked from the dormitories in the dark to the temple in the upper garden. But there was no escaping the heat at the ashram. The ceiling fans only circulated the burning hot air and high humidity.

In October of that year, the temperature was close to 100 degrees Fahrenheit. For me, this created a great physical challenge. My body weight had dropped to 95 pounds, which is dangerously thin for a 5-foot-10-inch woman. Still, I felt it was my duty to help maintain the ashram as a sacred place. I never once thought of leaving. In January, as the weather shifted, I slowly regained my previous healthy weight. I continued my spiritual practices along with the sacred duties we all performed together.

About six months later, I was reminded of what seemed to be one of my previous lifetimes, when Baba said to me, "Since you have been a beauty queen, you will help open a beauty shop." I smiled as I remembered my modeling job at the Scottsdale tea room when I was in the process of finding my true path.

I became part of the planning committee assigned to help other devotees create a shop in an as-yet-to-be-built structure across the street from the ashram. Many of the *adivasi*, the name for the original inhabitants of the region, came to help Baba and the other devotees by carrying rocks and sand to the building site. Several of the men living in the ashram had carpentry skills and helped with the construction. Inside the new store, they created cabinets for supplies and display items that might be of interest to patrons visiting the shop.

Baba sent me to Bombay, to purchase Indian finery that we could sell to visitors. The saris were made of the most beautiful colors of silk imaginable. During festive occasions, every color available was worn by the women, in great celebration. The shop also offered many variations of mala beads, made from specific sacred stones that would be of interest to those practicing meditation. We had many sets of rudrakshas, the same beads I saw in my first vision of Baba.

The colors, the culture, the spiritual practices had all infused my soul. This had become my way of life. While it was a joy to see many beautiful things, my attachment to them was minimal. The real goal was to provide services for the visitors, who would create resources to support the ashram. For instance, we had a husband and wife team living there who were hair stylists. Everyone got their hair cut in our shop, devotees as well as visitors.

While Baba insisted that each devotee provide some form of service toward maintaining the ashram, many other people with extensive learning shared their expertise while visiting. I learned various skills in the healing arts from some of these visitors, such as reflexology, Ayurvedic principles, and—of great interest to me—Vedic astrology.

Jyotisha, is the traditional branch of Hindu astrology, which includes the study of astronomy and numerology. Known as the *science of light*, the reading is provided by a Vedic astrologer, who recommends to the person receiving the reading certain jyotish gemstones— chosen on the basis of sacred astrological principles. The Vedic astrologer advises which stones should be worn according to the placement of the planets in one's birth chart. In this belief system, everything in the universe has a connecting energy. Wearing specific stones is a way to increase resonant self-expression.

I was skeptical. Could wearing a gemstone really provide protection, impart spiritual guidance, or convey important information about the future? However, in the study of jyotish, I learned that every particle in the universe has information in it. It reminded me of the words of William Blake who wrote, "To see a World in a Grain of Sand / And a Heaven in a Wild Flower."

I consulted with a Vedic astrologer who advised me that the planet Saturn was in an exalted place in my birth chart, which indicated that its influence on my life would be positive.

This, and the fact that Saturn is known as the "Lord of Karma," I interpreted to mean I would have a keen awareness of the lessons I needed to learn in this lifetime.

I once heard, "Enhance your strengths and manage your weaknesses." In the study of astrology, we are all influenced by the energy of the planets, to a greater or lesser degree. I decided to contemplate these concepts in meditation.

As I began, I asked for the wisdom of Saturn. I envisioned myself as part of the cosmos while all the other planets and stars vibrated their light around me. Then, I felt the beginning of the transmission of insight. The other planets moved into a geometric grid of light. Saturn, the exalted teacher, was the most prominent.

Tilting on its axis, the planet's outer ring passed close to me. It became a fluid rope of light. Reaching for it, I propelled myself upward, traveling through space and time. Spread out below me, I saw the possible scenarios I could choose for the unfolding of my life lessons. Saturn was providing me with the wisdom to help navigate my cosmic path. I awakened from the vision with a whole new level of understanding.

After the insights of my meditation, I was inspired to seek out the perfect stone to enhance Saturn's beneficial influence on my life. I was advised to choose a natural blue sapphire that I continue to wear (along with other gemstones that harmonize further planetary influences in my chart).

I am glad I purchased the pure untreated stones in India. Unlike many found in the United States, they came naturally from the earth and hadn't been altered by heat, radiation, or dyes to change their color or structure. This kind of treatment negates the natural healing properties of the stones and renders them useless for spiritual study and practice.

The study of jyotish reminded me of my grandparents and how they consulted the *Farmer's Almanac*. They used it to determine when to plant the fields, cut hair, and wean calves—all according to the path of the planets and most especially the influence of the moon. The use of Vedic astrology to aid with life's challenges is not so far removed from this concept. We must learn to harmonize the influences around us, thereby finding wisdom or, more specifically, the lessons to be learned. Sometimes answers can still be found in the *old ways*.

At this time, my ashram studies were focused on the Shiva Puranas, one of the many Sanskrit texts that focus on step-by-step yoga practices. Sometimes while meditating, in front of a large statue of Lord Shiva, I folded my hands at my heart while I recited Sanskrit prayers. During one particular vision, the statue came to life!

Lord Shiva reached down, took my folded hands and raised my body up to stand next to him. As Brahmin priests came into the room chanting mantras, he guided me by the arm and we encircled a small sacred fire several times, as couples do in Vedic wedding ceremonies. When we came to a stop, he presented me with a gift—a beautiful shawl.

As I gazed at it, I realized there was a *living* cobra woven into the fibers of the shawl. In sacred paintings of Lord Shiva, he was often depicted with a cobra wrapped around his neck, which was a symbol of protection. He reached forward to place the shawl around my shoulders. I was feeling grateful for the gift; yet, at the same time, I was fearful of the snake. As the shawl touched my body, the snake swung around and bit me on the left side of my neck, ending the meditation in a flash of light.

By this time, I was accustomed to having visions, but this one felt more like an initiation. It reminded me of the ecstatic vision of St. Theresa when she became the bride of

Christ. The euphoria of this experience extended from the spiritual realm into my life on the physical plane. A short time later, I had a realization that felt almost like déjà vu: one of the other devotees I knew was to become my future husband.

Mark was one of the first people I met in 1974, when I arrived at the retreat site in Albuquerque. He was to become my spiritual partner. His sister, the woman in the blue sari who first inspired me to learn meditation, also lived at the ashram. Mark said that while helping the other guests who were attending Baba's retreat that weekend, he remembered taking note of my name on the registration list. Once again, my first initiation with Baba continued to resonate throughout my life.

As my experiences at the ashram unfolded, Mark and I became every close, like spiritual brother and sister. We were joined in a colorful, traditional Vedic wedding ceremony, performed by Baba's Brahmin priest. During it, I remembered the dream of my marriage to Lord Shiva, which now made sense to me. Even though the dream was a symbol of my marriage to God, my wedding with Mark was the earthly manifestation of it. I knew then that our union would be a sacred one.

Unfortunately, Baba was recovering from an illness and was unable to attend. But while visiting him later, he showered us with his spiritual affection. We then spent a week in the honeymoon suite at Juhu Beach, outside of Bombay, savoring Baba's blessings. We took a ferry to an island to visit a sacred place called the Elephanta Caves, which heightened our blissful union. Afterward, we returned home to the ashram to live.

Although it was unusual, Baba made the decision to let us reside in a small house on the ashram premises. Generally, men and women lived in separate dormitories, even if they were married. He said he would allow this, only because we were practicing brahmacharya, a form of celibacy. We continued to follow Baba's teachings for the entire time we lived there. This part of our lives was reserved for spiritual development, which we were able to accomplish side by side. In 1980, after we had moved from the ashram and had started living in our own home, Mark and I had a child.

We were blessed with a beautiful baby girl. When she was born, we called Baba, to ask if we should give her a special name.

"That must be Kalyani," was his response.

And so we decided to include Kalyani in her formal name. It means blessed, auspicious, and beautiful. It is recognized as one of the many names of Goddess Parvati.

Even after leaving the ashram, we still tried to follow the teachings and practices Baba had given to us. This was much more difficult in the so-called *real* world. There was no group effort to support a meditation practice, whereas in the ashram there was a regimented schedule where spiritual practices were required. Regardless, we did our best to carry our beliefs into society and everyday life.

As someone who had just come out of a communal living experience at the ashram, I found it difficult to meet expenses. This was a time when the practice of yoga was just starting to take hold in our culture. So to make a living, I taught classes in yoga asana and meditation. However, this barely paid the bills. I had little time for my own spiritual practice, and I was striving to do well at being a new mother. In the ashram, each person was there to support the others and the higher vision. At times, in this new life, I felt very much alone.

In 1983, I accepted an executive position in the beauty and fragrance division at Christian Dior. I turned to this field, in part, because it was work I was comfortable with, and I was confident I could be successful with a well-known beauty and skincare corporation. Everyone was struggling to make money at the time, but I felt certain that the high-end fashion industry would continue to flourish.

It was also becoming obvious to me that my marriage was no longer working out. I was soon to become a single mother. Mark and I weren't responding well to the economic strains and stresses of no longer living in the ashram under Baba's wings. In 1985, a job in the career Mark wanted became available in another part of the country. After much discussion and with great sadness, we decided to go our separate ways.

It is important to know that we have remained close. There is still a *soul connection* there. We continue to share in the life of our beautiful daughter and her children to this day. Sometimes in this life, however, our time with another person comes to completion. Our contract together is fulfilled, and the lessons for us to learn are completed.

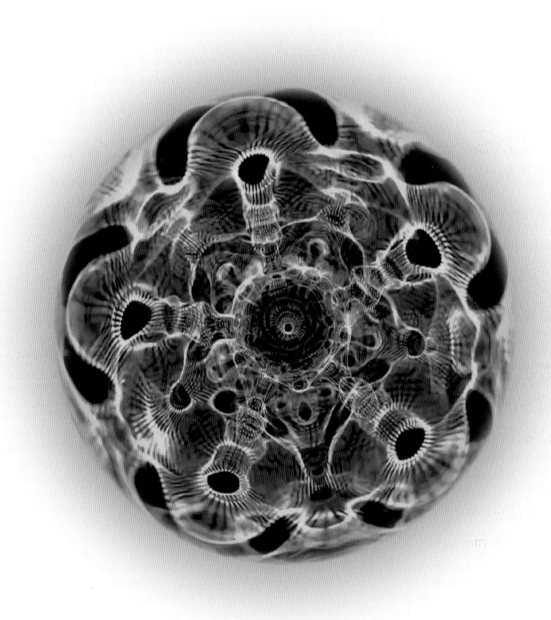

Chapter Two

Signs of a New Direction

*M*y work in the world of beauty was financially successful and in many ways rewarding. As a beauty executive, I was given the opportunity to enjoy spa treatments and other retreat experiences. This led me to the realization there were techniques that could improve health while addressing the desire for natural beauty or cosmetic enhancements.

While living at the ashram, I had learned many health and wellness techniques. I found it interesting that some of the ancient healing secrets were beginning to be considered valuable by traditional medical offices. This, along with the need I felt to communicate the importance of health in the full expression of beauty, aided me in my decision to open a consulting business to help doctors find alternative choices—like massage, acupuncture, and other similar healing techniques—to add to their practices.

As I made connections with medical offices, I would often learn about new diagnostic tools that were on the forefront of research. Noninvasive techniques were being created as less dangerous alternatives for finding possible problems in the body. In 1997, I was attending a health conference in Florida where I learned about a new scanning device, a way of discovering disturbances in the body, called *thermography*. It was an alternative to mammograms, which many women found painful and stressful, to detect breast cancer. This fostered my interest in tools that could show cellular changes in the body. I wanted to know more about techniques that were noninvasive and wouldn't risk causing further illness.

In 2001, I was building my consulting business with doctors and healthcare professionals. It wasn't unusual for practitioners of alternative therapies to call, asking how they might offer their services to physicians. Then one day the phone rang—it was the call that would change my life. Initially, I inquired about the caller's background, to learn if he had any skills that could help my clients. My inquiry led to a fascinating conversation about yoga, therapeutic massage, and sound therapy. When he mentioned therapeutic sound, I asked what technique he worked with.

He told me about Dr. Peter Guy Manners, a British osteopath, who was using sound therapy very successfully by means of a sound generating device. The caller had apprenticed with Dr. Manners and was the first person to introduce me to the word "cymatics." Toward the end of the conversation, he mentioned that the doctor was in his 90s, and someone should go learn his work before he was no longer able to teach it. I asked the caller how I could help him.

He said, "I don't know. I just think someone needs to be aware of Dr. Manners' work before he decides to retire."

During the conversation, as the caller talked about sound, I had a profound physical awareness—my own memories of sound experiences played before my eyes. In my life, I had relied upon Gregorian chant and Sanskrit as the tools for activating energy within me. He spoke about an instrument that made these kinds of experiences possible for everyone. I was catapulted into a dual reality. I was struck with the realization that everything important I had done in this life had led me to this conversation.

When I was growing up, if I was sick and the medical doctor in the community was not available, my mother would take us to the local osteopath, which always resulted in an interesting visit. We used to visit "Old Doc Ann," who would lay us on a table and examine us in a kind and loving way, sometimes massaging our bones but always causing lots of giggles. She never gave us a shot with a needle or did anything to cause us pain. So I was certainly intrigued by the idea that an instrument for sound healing could be available through an osteopath. I suspected there might be some special kind of healing involved in Dr. Manners' practices.

When I heard the click of the receiver ending the call, my whole world was altered. My depth perception shifted. The wall in front of me blew out. There, before me, was another plane of existence. I was on solid ground, but where the wall had been, a brilliance appeared. I was observing the radiance but felt part of it at the same time.

A great light flooded in, but to name all of the colors accurately would be impossible. I can only best describe a few of them as the most radiant ruby, the brightest luminescent yellow, and the deepest emerald green. Then right before me, manifesting from the light, an angelic being appeared! Then every color of the spectrum was revealed, full of vibrancy and power. The wings of the angel engulfed me. They were within me and all around me.

This was the messenger I had been waiting for.

The experience may have lasted for only a few moments—or maybe much longer. It was difficult to define in terms of time. Then I felt a very strong tap on my middle back, pushing me forward. The vision ended, but the feeling I was being guided onward continued. This visitation was one I couldn't turn away from. From that moment, I had to know more about Dr. Peter Guy Manners and cymatic therapy.

A few days later after the elation had subsided, even though I knew I needed to go meet Dr. Manners, my heart and soul became clouded in self-doubt. I realized the whole angel experience was something I needed to keep to myself. I was aware of the power of the naysayer to deter those who are embarking on a great journey. Not everyone believes in angelic messengers, let alone that we should act on what they might ask us to do. So I was hesitant to discuss it with anyone.

Since I had never heard of Dr. Manners, or cymatics, I immediately searched for information on the internet. My first find regarding cymatics was a Swiss scientist Hans Jenny. He created *sound images*. I was fascinated by them and couldn't wait to find out more. Dr. Jenny was a medical doctor and a visual artist, who chose to create *cymatic imagery* from an artistic perspective, rather than a scientific or medical one. I was very interested in it all.

In addition, I found information that led me to Jeff Volk. He was an American publisher, with great connections to other scientists and writers, and was considered to be an expert in the field of cymatics. Interestingly, he had commissioned a translation into English of the book *Cymatics* by Hans Jenny. He had also made an award-winning documentary film on the subject, called *Of Sound Mind and Body*.

While watching the documentary, I saw Dr. Manners for the first time. He had been filmed during one of the very few visits he made to America. As I watched his interview, I became more and more intrigued, because it was the first time I had ever seen sound being applied to the body. The experience of watching Jeff Volk's movie truly inspired me to go meet Dr. Manners and learn from him.

I found the doctor's phone number on the internet, and with no prior introduction, I called him out of the blue. His receptionist answered. When I asked to speak to him, there was no hesitation or any questions about my identity. She quickly called him to the phone.

In a very proper British accent, I heard, "Hello. This is Dr. Manners."

I told him who I was and that I was interested in his therapy. I had many questions, some of which I am sure he had heard before. I wanted to know exactly how he was doing *sound therapy*, and what kind of technology he was using. But what I really wanted to know was the kind of success he was having.

"What about cancer?" I asked hopefully.

"No," he replied, to my dismay, "we don't treat cancer. That is the work of oncologists."

I also wanted to ask questions of a metaphysical kind, but refrained from doing so. The whole exchange was very proper, very professional. At the end of our conversation, we agreed I would come to the clinic in Bretforton, England, to learn about his technique. However, he insisted that if I were to do so, I would need to sign up for his training. Then he inquired about my medical background.

"I don't have any medical degrees," I said hesitantly.

"You will need to know anatomy and physiology," he insisted.

"I have a working knowledge of the basics of Chinese medicine and Ayurveda," I replied. "I will come with a good understanding of the body."

"That will help you," he concluded.

When the conversation ended, I felt elated: I was going forward with my vision! I continued to research Dr. Manners and cymatics until the time I was to leave for the United Kingdom. After I learned more about the therapy, I decided to order one of his devices in advance. When I called him back, he quoted me a price of 5000 American dollars. He promised that it would be ready upon my arrival.

Then, one week before I was to leave for Bretforton, I received a phone call from him at around 4 a.m. When I answered, he said, "This is Dr. Peter Guy Manners in the United Kingdom. Where are you? I thought you were coming to my clinic."

It took me a moment to focus, and then I spoke slowly, "Oh… No, Dr. Manners. My ticket is for next week. I was planning to come to the clinic then." There was a brief silence, then he apologized and quickly hung up.

In a way, I was excited by the call, because it seemed he was sincerely interested in me coming to visit. On the other hand, I wondered how he could have made that mistake. I could only imagine the other challenges I might have to face with an elderly doctor in a foreign country while learning about a therapy hardly anyone knew anything about.

I made the trip for the ten-day training with two other women who were friends, and who I felt would give me their truthful, insightful impressions of Dr. Manners and the therapy he was providing. I trusted their combined backgrounds would give me a broader viewpoint of what we were about to experience.

One of my friends was a nurse with an extensive medical background. She was also somewhat open to alternatives to traditional medicine. The other woman was a medical intuitive and psychic. I wanted to look at all aspects of *sound healing*, as it was sometimes referred to.

When we first walked into the clinic wearing our white lab coats (which we had been instructed to bring), we were warmly greeted by the staff. This place was different than any other medical office I had ever been to. As we began the tour of the facility, conducted by one of the clinicians, there was a general feeling that the clients and the staff were sincerely glad to be there.

His office, the Bretforton Clinic, was housed in an old historic building on the main floor. Inside, the waiting room looked more like a spa with a beautiful indoor fountain. It was otherwise modestly furnished, with seating for five patients. There were few decorative aspects, other than several bouquets of fake flowers arranged in vases and placed around the room. Literature about the facility had indicated there was a swimming pool. We were interested to see how it might be utilized. It was located behind the clinic in a greenhouse-like structure; this was also included in the tour.

When we returned back to the main facility, Dr. Manners appeared. People often ask me for my first impression of him. Due to the documentary I had watched, our meeting at the clinic wasn't my first time seeing him. From the video, I had already determined that he looked great for a 97-year-old man. In person, his energy was amazing. He had bright eyes, a full head of hair, and was very agile (even when compared to a man much younger than he).

He was successfully managing the clinic, training other practitioners, and caring for many patients each day. He wore a white jacket and pants, as did his staff of therapists and trainees. This was customary for osteopathic doctors. There were also massage therapists in the office who assisted Dr. Manners after sound therapy had been administered.

It was only when I saw him in person, that I realized how short he was. I sensed that he was uncomfortable when we first met, because I am 5 foot 10, and he was probably 5 foot 4. He appeared anxious for me to take a seat. I did so, and after that first visit, I always tried to make him feel at ease, especially when speaking about serious matters.

The instruction we received was conducted upstairs in Dr. Manners' study, even though we were told there was a larger room downstairs that was the official classroom. The study, meanwhile, was located next to what had been his laboratory. This was always locked. We were told no one was permitted to go in there. This was the rule because of traumatic events we were to learn about later.

On the first day, we began the training. All three of us were required to take it, regardless of our backgrounds. In his clinic, as opposed to an American medical center, only cymatic therapy was being taught and practiced. When he appeared, he had three other people with him. (It was my understanding that there were many practitioners who worked there daily—some in training, and some who had been working with him for quite a while.)

While we were seated in the study, we were offered twenty to thirty small booklets to read. The pamphlets were on various health-related and esoteric topics. The front covers were stamped with the words "Property of Bretforton Clinic." Some of the titles included: "The Spirit of Medicine: Uniting Science and Medicine," "Electrobiodynamics," "Cymatic Treatment for the New Age of Medicine," and "Cymatics and the Einsteinian Theory." They were compiled by Dr. Manners.

Some of the text seemed strangely familiar. Perhaps it was pertinent information merely collated by him to create our complete course of study. Surprisingly, these were the only written texts offered for our certification process. We found this to be somewhat disappointing.

Occasionally, he would drop by the study to see if we had any questions on what we were reading. The first time, we asked what further training would be provided. His answer was simply that we needed to fully understand the material we had just been given.

Sometimes, I would get the opportunity to ask my own questions. "Has there ever been any adverse effects from using cymatic therapy?"

"No. It's all audible sound in the lower hearing range. These frequencies are most effective when used transdermally and applied with an applicator," he answered.

"I know there are some other frequencies and sound therapy instruments in the market place. Is this like the Rife machine?" I asked.

"Oh no," he replied. "This is nothing like that. Most of Rife's frequencies are not audible. His are designed to destroy pathogens, while cymatic therapy supports the body. The majority of what are called "cymatic codes," which are generated from the device, contain five frequencies and can be used on a daily basis."

"But, why five frequencies?"

"Because they worked," he answered. "We tried combining two, three, and almost gave up. It was when we put five together that we began to have great results."

"How did you measure the five frequencies? Did you have five generators? What instrumentation did you have?" Many questions came tumbling forth when he was in the room with us. I thought I needed to ask as many questions as possible, since we were unsure about what would be included in the rest of our training.

"We had instruments that are no longer available. They were all destroyed in Germany after the war."

I was trying to process everything he was telling me. Did he really mean that someone had created a type of pitch pipe that could call all the cells of the body back into harmony? Did he, Dr. Manners, really hold the secret to vibro-acoustically aligning the body? When I asked a lot of questions, he appeared to become uncomfortable. He would talk very fast and respond in a condescending manner. In my mind, I was asking fair questions that other people must have asked before. I was beginning to see that sometimes great possibilities are coupled with serious doubts about the person providing them.

Occasionally, when I thought his answers were incomplete (or that he was avoiding my questions altogether), I reminded myself that we had yet to establish a relationship based on trust. Still, there were times when I couldn't help myself, and I would continue to press for answers.

"What were the first cases you had success with?" I inquired. I wanted more concrete information, hoping there would be a condition I could observe.

"We saw inflammation and swelling disappear," he offered. "We also noted that bone fractures were healing much faster. There were marked improvements in skin diseases. Because we were having these successes, we decided to study other aspects of the body." According to him, his ability to work on numerous conditions was a result of his participation in more than forty years of research.

Regardless of the doubt I felt when he was answering our initial questions, it disappeared when I saw him work with the patients. They all responded very favorably to his therapy and reported feeling better after each session. The more I watched and listened, the more I found myself believing in him again.

At other times, I would inquire about his credentials on the wall, trying to get a better idea about his education and where his techniques had originated. They seemed more like certificates of attendance rather than diplomas. This prompted me to ask him where he studied medicine.

He replied, "St. Thomas Hospital in London. There is no diploma on the wall because many of my records were destroyed during the war."

I was still having difficulty understanding how he made the transition from being a traditional medical doctor to becoming a researcher of sound frequencies. His response was that his medical school advisors had told him his personality was better suited for going into research. Then, after the war in the late 1940s, he claimed to have found a job in a laboratory with German scientists who were doing research with sound. He learned they were studying the effect of sound on medical conditions, and this interested him.

At this point in his story, the details became sketchy, and he was unwilling to give me any names. He appeared to have a fear that some ill would befall his contemporaries if he revealed who they were.

One day, when he and I were alone, I asked the same questions again. This time, there was one name he mentioned: Dr. Brauner. Dr. Manners had become close with him, but had lost track of him over the years. In subsequent days, I tried to find out more with additional questions but with no success. No amount of pressing afforded me any further information. This did nothing to calm my fears; though at a certain point, if I were to proceed with my education, I had to let go of questioning him any further. I decided to try and create more situations in the future where I could have time alone with him.

At the end of the first day, we thanked Dr. Manners for the opportunity to study with him and cordially said our goodbyes. However, the conversation on the way back to the hotel was filled with conflicting observations. His reticence to answer our questions and the sparse amount of written materials had us wondering.

We witnessed many people have physical healing experiences, but we wanted to understand how it was happening. There were still a lot of unanswered questions, and I needed the technique to be validated. Still, I had to admit that the whole day held a strong fascination for me. I felt a wonderful excitement building about the days ahead.

On the second day, I was anxious to see the device I had ordered and already paid for. When I asked Dr. Manners about it, he informed me it wasn't ready yet. I did notice over the next few days, around 2:30 p.m., a gentleman arrived and was taken into the doctor's private office. Repeatedly, these meetings resulted in an exchange of loud voices, which sounded like arguing. I came to understand that this was the man who constructed Dr. Manners' devices. Not only was there a delay with manufacturing, but there were also some questionable business practices going on as well. From their tones, there was certainly trouble brewing between them. This was a disturbing thought for me. I still hadn't received my own device. I also began to wonder if it would ever be possible to get larger numbers of them for use throughout the United States.

Now, while I was fascinated with his therapy, the devices I saw him working with resembled old radio transmitters or outdated computers. This didn't look like a technology that would be accepted in the United States, nor a device that could provide the medicine of the future. I was looking for another solution. Since he was getting closer to the end of his career, it was obvious to me that no further research or development was going to happen with him.

Still, we continued to focus on our studies and observe the treatments going on in the clinic. We were there to learn as much as possible. But by the fifth day, when I hadn't received the device, I decided to ask Dr. Manners to meet me for dinner. I needed to find out the real story. The scene unfolding before me was of an aging British osteopath who had an amazing form of sound therapy, which would be lost to the world if not brought forward through a bigger, better plan.

Later that evening, he brought his nurse Doreen to dinner with us. When we first sat down at the table, the talk was pleasant. I noticed that Dr. Manners started to relax and was quietly staring down at the table. Moments later, something strange happened. The spoons started to bend into unusual shapes, as if some outside force was suddenly at work at our table!

"Stop it! Don't do that!" Doreen exclaimed. "The restaurant manager said he will throw us out if you keep making this happen!"

"Wow! How did you do that?" I asked excitedly, hardly able to believe my eyes. "Can you teach me how to do it?"

"I really don't know how I do it," he replied, looking somewhat bewildered. "I just relax. When I get into a certain state of mind, it happens."

"Please don't do this," Doreen interrupted. "We won't have any place to go out and eat anymore."

It was clear this was the wrong time to ask, but my mind was racing. How could he possibly have bent the silverware just by looking at it? This esoteric phenomenon was totally unexpected. I am usually open to the unexplainable, but this was completely astonishing. Regardless, I was surprised by how much I really wanted to believe in his mystical abilities.

I couldn't wait to see what else he might manifest.

Meanwhile, we were forced to hide the silverware under the table until we could straighten it out. To my dismay, after placing it back on the table, there was no more discussion about his unusual talent. The three of us acted as if nothing had happened. Everything returned to normal as we ordered our dinner.

I know there are probably a lot of people who simply won't believe this happened. Personally, I have encountered many things that raise questions about the findings of science and the laws of physics, so it wasn't impossible for me to believe what I had seen. This silverware episode made me wonder how often we keep ourselves from new discoveries because of our limited thinking. I was beginning to suspect that Dr. Manners had the power to change our perceptions about a lot of things. I decided to wait and ask him about it again later.

We enjoyed the meal and shared some polite conversation. I waited until I thought it was appropriate, and then I spoke. "Dr. Manners, it is my observation that you are having some trouble with your manufacturing. Is that true?"

Very quickly, it was obvious to me that he didn't like the question. His body language showed he wasn't prepared to answer. Still, after a short pause, I couldn't help myself and continued to press him.

"I know I could help you, if you would consider bringing your therapy to the United States," I offered.

"Oh," he responded, with a great sense of relief. "I have been waiting for you!"

I didn't believe he meant he had been waiting for me personally. I had seen his great frustration with the current manufacturing, and even though his therapy was relatively new, his devices were very outdated. Both issues could certainly impact the efficacy of his therapy and whether the concept would be accepted by—or available to—more people. He seemed ready to talk to anyone about other possibilities.

"As I have mentioned, Dr. Manners, I have a healthcare consulting business which could connect us to many people who could help promote your therapy. There might be new technology I could introduce you to as well."

"Before we discuss this, I must be assured the integrity of the frequencies will be maintained, and the wave patterns will not be manipulated," he replied. This comment made me wonder if there had been previous attempts to alter his healing frequencies or his approach to the therapy. I had to acknowledge we still didn't know each other very well.

"Oh, I can certainly understand," I responded. "We will discuss this more thoroughly and make sure everyone's interests will be protected."

The dinner ended on a high note with a very positive new aspect to our relationship. From that moment on, I could see the next part of the story unfolding. I knew I would continue to visit him in the United Kingdom. I also experienced a future vision of him coming to the United States. There were great life changes coming.

The experience of the first phone call about Dr. Manners was still very much with me. Somehow, with no prior experience of this healing treatment, I knew I was supposed to help him bring cymatic therapy into the future. I believe there are angels around me all the time, messengers that offer guidance, but I had never experienced a visitation quite like the one I had after that phone call regarding Dr. Manners. I still had the feeling I was being powerfully pushed forward.

The remaining days with him were filled with amazing observations. Throughout the whole visit, I saw myself as an investigator with a very healthy skepticism. I wanted to believe that cymatic therapy was a great healing tool for everyone, but I was there looking for truth. I wanted proof. I hoped Dr. Manners could show this to me.

One of the most profound experiences we had at the clinic took place in the swimming pool. Before visiting, we had seen a picture of it in the clinic's pamphlet, but the brochure hadn't explained the water was charged with the same frequencies used to treat Dr. Manners' patients.

Somehow, they were being transmitted into the pool by a system behind the wall where the water was flowing in. During our initial ten-day visit, the exact mechanism for how it worked wasn't shown to us. But the water felt very warm and silky to me, and it looked incredibly clear. Everyone felt physically buoyant in it. Many of the patients used it as part of their therapy and reported that their aches and pains were disappearing, much like they would in a mineral spring.

I noticed there was no smell of chlorine; I asked Dr. Manners if he used any chemicals in the pool.

"There is no need for that," he replied. "The frequencies prevent any problems. There is nothing bad growing in the water."

After we had been in the pool the first time, we went back as often as we could. We all experienced various healing responses in it, just like his other patients. One of my traveling companions, after three consecutive days of being in the pool, had amazing relief from excruciating pain and inflammation in the scar tissue on her shoulder from a previous surgery. She could finally stop wearing the bandages over the keloid tissue area that had plagued her for years.

I had no specific health challenges back then, but I couldn't wait to experience the buoyancy I felt in my body each time I went in the pool. It was deeply relaxing. As for the building itself: it smelled more like the scents used in aromatherapy, though no one fragrance could be identified; it was a very pleasant temperature indoors, even in the heat of the summer; and there was no sound, other than the voices of those enjoying the experience.

Another important aspect of those last few days, was being able to observe Dr. Manners with his patients. It was on a limited basis, since we were in training, but I did witness he had more than one persona when he worked with people. It was then I saw his true *healer self* emerge. As a doctor, with his patients, a completely different personality showed itself. The way he touched people, the way he listened, and how he was able to help them was the deciding factor for me to bring his therapy to those who were suffering in the United States.

I never witnessed what you would call healing miracles. Instead, I saw people steadily improving from the pure experience of sound. Everyone we observed in his thirty-minute sessions always said they felt better at the end of them. During my introductory visit to the clinic, I saw him treat approximately twenty-five clients with cymatic therapy. On my subsequent visits to the United Kingdom, I accompanied him while he administered treatment to many other patients. I viewed some of their records, still looking for proof of the therapy's efficacy (of course, only after we had confirmed a legal business relationship).

At the end of our ten-day experience, my friends and I were given a certificate of attendance in the study of Cymatic BioEnergetic Medicine. The rest of the certification to become a *cymatic therapy practitioner* consisted of developing case studies, writing papers, and consulting with Dr. Manners on the treatment of clients.

Even though I studied with him at his clinic, received his certification, and consulted with him on numerous cases over the years, I never became a practitioner as a profession. I did, however, receive a diploma from him for my doctorate in Cymatic BioEnergetic Medicine.

I always felt that my responsibility was to bring the therapy to many. My dream was to make Cymatherapy a household word. That responsibility has always taken precedence over any personal aspirations I might have had to become a practitioner.

The only downside of the last few days of our visit was his continued unwillingness to answer my questions. The more I pressed him, the less his answers satisfied me. One of the questions I asked was whether he had hospital privileges. He replied somewhat indignantly, "I don't need them because there are no hospitals around here."

While his comment was true, it did nothing to assuage my fears about his background and where all the frequencies had come from. I had to remember that not all doctors are granted such privileges, nor do they need them. However, if I couldn't be sure of his credentials or where his information had originated, I wasn't sure I should invest my resources (and my life) to promote his work. And there was no way to prove anything without his cooperation.

He did, however, share a story with me later. The Germans, whom he identified as Nazis, had invaded the laboratory where he worked. Surprisingly, this happened after the war and long after the time when there was any danger for an Englishman to be in Germany. But he claimed he escaped the raid on the lab unscathed due in part to his Aryan looks and the fact that he had not been forced to respond to any questions with his British accent. This invasion supposedly destroyed much of the research on the frequencies he was using in the clinic—not to mention the specific devices which had been used to do the research and provide the treatment. He said some of the scientists had escaped, but with only part of the research.

This I found difficult to accept. How could all the instruments be gone? Why hadn't he tried to replace them? How could all the researchers be gone? Was there no one else left doing this work? With results this incredible, why didn't he try to find the others? In the United States, this lack of proof would be unacceptable. I questioned him many times and the answer was always the same.

"Oh no, it would be trouble for them. Everything was destroyed."

At times, I wondered if his reluctance to share these details was due to several traumatic events that had occurred. Including a threat upon his life in 1989, when part of his own research laboratory in Bretforton was destroyed by fire while he was living there. The flames, interestingly, only consumed the research part of the laboratory. He chose not to reveal this information to me until later in our relationship. All I did know was even the staff said he never allowed anyone to look inside. This explained why the laboratory was locked on our first visit and continued to be for as long as I knew him.

He was never able to tell me who he thought had done it or why. However, he did say he was given British police protection following the fire, which was thought to have been caused by a bomb. I couldn't help but wonder who would want to prevent his research from being available to others. What could their motivation be?

There was also the loss of his wife, Maria—the love of his life—in 1991. Clearly those couple of years had been a very challenging time for him. His emotionless responses to questions about this period were always difficult to figure out. He may have been suffering from symptoms caused by an emotional trauma. Watching his eyes you could see he was revisiting some painful memories he didn't want to talk about. If I continued to press him, he would completely shut down. I also had to consider the idea that, no matter what the circumstances, he was simply unwilling to share certain details with me.

To give him the benefit of the doubt, he had no way of knowing what I would do with the information he relinquished to me. Whenever I tried to speak with him about any of the formerly mentioned traumatic events, he would become obstinate and simply refuse to answer any questions. This would only make me wonder what he was hiding. Why was he was refusing to tell the truth?

Then I would remind myself to try and understand his resistance, to remember the overwhelming emotions of what he had been through. However, it was hard to trust in the knowledge he was giving, in the midst of the history he was withholding. Many times, I had to walk away with no answers.

While some people found Dr. Manners eccentric and difficult to work with, I always felt compelled to stay the course. Each time I was ready to give up, I would experience the same angelic force that sent me to learn from him. It was the same tap on my back—the same pressure to move forward. In the end, I can't fill all the holes in his story or find the sources of his information, but I have finally found peace in my own conclusion. I choose to believe he was simply the last living messenger of a collaborative group who first discovered these amazing sound secrets.

Chapter Three

Steps of Faith

Regardless of whether I believed all of his story, the initial time I spent with Dr. Manners provided me with profound insights into a world of possibilities regarding the use of therapeutic sound. After our first ten-day meeting, I returned home with the device I purchased from him, which I had seen him use with his patients (so I knew it worked). I began to assemble my manufacturing team through connections I already had. Admittedly, I had no previous experience with building devices; yet, somehow, I felt certain I could complete the task. Even though not all of my questions were answered, I had witnessed many people who experienced the relief of their pain. Observing the joy they felt at being able to go on with their lives, inspired me to offer this therapy to everyone. What I saw happen with Dr. Manners and his patients was truly incredible.

Many people have asked me how I got started spreading the word. It was actually very simple. I explained to my friends I had a new device that could help health challenges using noninvasive sound. Then, some of my neighbors trusted me enough to give it a try. The next thing I knew, their friends came to see me. Even with my limited cymatic therapy experience and training, I was developing a reputation for being able to help people.

People with chronic aches-and-pains and stress-related problems came to see me. Even those with serious illnesses came to find out if sound could have some positive effect. I met many people looking for answers that traditional medicine didn't always have. With each case, I became more convinced that the therapy worked. My first clients in the United States were extremely valuable in my personal quest. The people who were willing to try this new therapy, this new way of thinking, confirmed for me the importance of bringing cymatic therapy to America.

I was certainly on the proving ground. What I had learned in the studies of Ayurvedic principles, and in some of the tenets of Chinese medicine, had given me knowledge that was a great addition to the minimal clinical training Dr. Manners provided. He had been adamant in his view that I needed traditional medical training. But my results with clients using techniques from my own background proved incredible.

My intuition told me there must be some relationship between his therapy and the ancient systems. This could explain why he found the combination of five frequencies as one of the reasons for his successes. The significance of the number five is prevalent in the Vedic and Chinese traditions. Both of these systems state our physical and subtle bodies are interwoven with sound and light. Each philosophy has powerful sounds to activate our *prana* or *chi* fields.

Within these systems, there are many correspondences that can be threaded through specific five syllable mantras, five subtle bodies, five elements, and the ancient marma and acupuncture points. I think that having an awareness of five in our natural world and honoring the harmony it presents in the universe is an important correlation to this form of healing.

As my success continued, I began to wonder if the average person could care for themselves, meeting many of their own health challenges, by using this therapy. The more I worked with clients, it was evident every one of them was helped in some way. How could it be that one device brought so much benefit to everyone, I wondered.

From this period of time, I have many incredible stories of the miraculous results I was hoping for. The doubts I had been plagued with during my initial meetings with Dr. Manners were starting to disappear. However, there were also experiences that made me realize the magnitude of my claims. I had taken on a huge personal responsibility.

My agreement with my new clients was I would provide a thirty-minute session at no charge. In exchange, they were to contact me by phone or email within twenty-four hours to let me know of any changes in their pain or stress levels, as well as sleep patterns. They were also to inform me of any other reduction of symptoms they experienced. I required all of my recruits to fill out a health history form. During which, I asked many questions so I could really find out about the person I was trying to help.

One of my clients was a woman who had survived a double mastectomy and was now in remission; however, she had incredible pain due to the staples that attached her reconstructed breasts to her chest. She had been suffering with this pain for over a year.

I asked her to lay down on the massage table, and I began to administer the sound therapy to her body with an applicator, close to the areas where she felt the most pain. I also applied it along the corresponding meridian pathways, to help move the energy away from her areas of soreness.

At the end of her thirty-minute session, I helped her sit up on the table. She said she felt dizzy, so I accompanied her to a seat in my living room and offered her a glass of water. She stayed there relaxing for another couple of hours. In the meantime, I was working on other people who had come to experience the cymatic therapy.

Finally she said, "I think I can go now."

I reminded her to contact me within the next twenty-four hours to report on her responses to the therapy. I used various grounding techniques to prepare her to get behind the wheel. However, when I saw her get into a bright-red BMW sports car, I started having some trepidation.

Two days later, I still hadn't heard from her. I was very concerned. I tried to call the number listed on her health history, but there was no answer. I spent the whole day wondering what could have gone wrong. On the third day, I called again; this time she answered.

"How are you feeling? What happened after your session?" I asked anxiously. "I was hoping to hear from you."

"I had the most amazing experience with the sound therapy!" she exclaimed. "As I was driving home, I decided to go to my art studio instead. I ended up staying there. I've been painting for three straight days, and I've been pain free!"

She explained that during those days she had completed her entire fall collection of paintings. Even more interestingly, she revealed they were all of the Buddha. Not only was she out of pain, but she also had what many would describe as a spiritual experience.

Throughout the years, I have received phone calls and emails from people who have chosen to share their personal experiences with Cymatherapy. I have been approached at many public lectures by people who can't wait to tell me the great benefits they have experienced with therapeutic sound.

A woman in Austin, Texas, described the Cymatherapy experience she had with a local practitioner: "During my session, I quickly fell into a very deep meditation. In a vision, I saw the hand of God placed on my head." The sound activated what she was ready to receive—the next step in her own journey to optimum health.

Shortly after, I found out she had an astrology practice. She guided her clients by integrating both Vedic and western astrological cycles. I had never met anyone proficient in both systems, so I made an appointment with her for a consultation. During the session, I learned many important things about the influences around me and the potential effect of the cycles on my personal growth. It was like revisiting one of my awakenings in India. Once again, I was shown the importance of ancient teachings and how they are connected to our healing today.

Sound therapy is life changing for many others; their experiences are profound on a physical, mental, and emotional level. All aspects of a person respond to these frequencies. With the successes I achieved while helping my first clients, I felt confident in bringing this form of therapy to the United States.

Although I had seen Dr. Manners administer sound therapy to many clients, I needed to believe that I was doing it as effectively. Was his kind of success always duplicatable? Dr. Manners hadn't been able to provide me with any scientific studies; I only had the anecdotal stories of his patients and my clients. He *had* told me the cymatic therapy device was a serious instrument, and it should not be placed in the hands of the untrained.

While I agreed with his idea that a practitioner would need a good understanding of how the body works in order to be proficient in utilizing the codes in his training, I also believed that with self-discipline and concerted study, others could grasp the concepts. I wanted to be able to train practitioners to carry the work forward. I believed that my studies in Chinese medicine and Ayurveda actually informed me of new ways to apply the therapy, and I was inspired to help others learn how to do it.

At the same time, I knew the ancient techniques were not endorsed by the traditional medical system prevalent in the United States. I wanted *everyone* to be able to access the power of sound for their own healing. But I also wondered, "Who would share my perceptions about any of these ideas? Who would believe my experiences?" I had no one to share my process with; I was forced to rely on myself in every way.

Next on the list was the creation of a new device. It was decided that Dr. Manners wouldn't be my collaborator on this aspect, because much had changed in the world of technology since the invention of his early instruments. His device would have required numerous upgrades and most likely a whole new design. We had to start from scratch.

He wasn't in a position to advise my team on creating a product that would administer advanced sound technology. He was only interested in being a doctor who could help people, not a designer of a device. Though he *was* concerned with protecting the integrity of the frequencies he had researched and worked with so effectively. Even though he wasn't directly involved in the actual production, I always kept him updated on the new device and honored the part he played in its evolution.

There was also the issue of funding for product development as well as the actual manufacturing. Then, even if I succeeded in creating a new device, who would I market it to? I knew I was putting myself at risk in numerous ways. There was no question I would need legal advice. A patent attorney would be required to protect my intellectual property, and I would need assistance in protecting my assets: a tax attorney, liability insurance, and maybe even malpractice protection as well. My list of concerns continued to grow.

Even with all the challenges, it was still hard not to tell people about this great new possibility for healing. However, I had to keep the ideas close to me so as not to dissipate the energy before it had a chance to manifest.

There was also another struggle going on in my mind: was this idea before its time? Would this be too big a leap in thinking? I was hoping people might relate cymatic therapy to regular ultrasound, using the idea of the latter as a bridge to lead to the acceptance of audible sound as a viable therapy.

I was also considering the ways this could positively affect my consulting business. I interviewed my clients about the use of therapeutic sound to find out how much they knew about it, and whether or not they would consider it as an alternative therapy. I knew medical offices were starting to be receptive to the use of laser and LED devices, so I believed the ground was fertile for planting new ideas in sound technology.

I envisioned a future in which we would all realize the power of sound. The tenets of energy medicine, how the body works as a whole system, helped me believe in Dr. Manners' principles of healing. All of my studies had given me reason to believe in sound as an incredible tool. I knew I needed to create an easy-to-use device that could help thousands. Despite the challenges, I was inspired to do so.

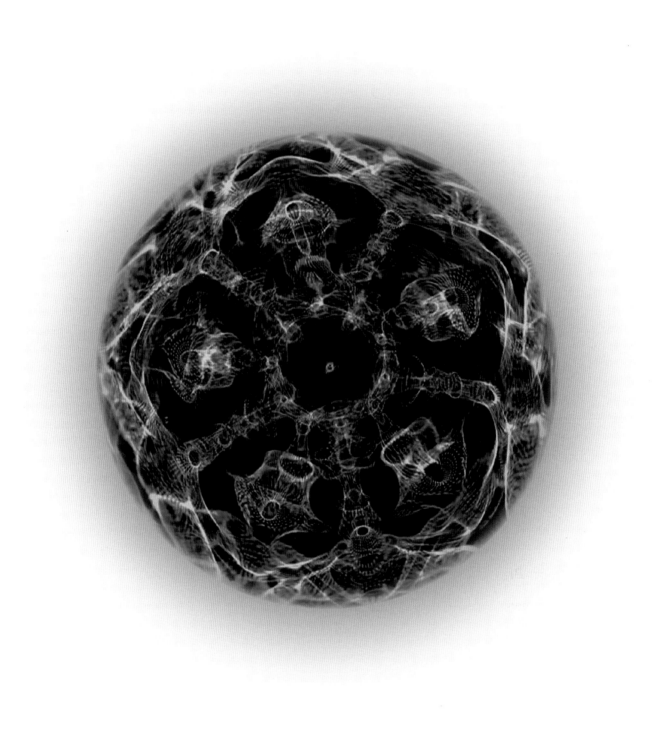

Chapter Four

The Implosion

*F*ollowing our meeting in 2001, I was still conferring with Dr. Manners on my initial cases. During our consultations, though we were an ocean apart, I could feel the teacher/student aspect of our relationship deepening.

That said, I had moved into the computer age, and he hadn't. He was unwilling to give up his fax machine, which was how we shared many of our communications. My fax machine was old and still required the use of thermal rolls, but since that was his favorite form of transatlantic communication, I continued to use it. I saved the most important faxes. Some of them were just about business, but I found many of them endearing. It was such a treat to receive the answers to my many questions, in his perfect handwriting.

In these messages, with his carefully detailed and explicit instructions, I felt a genuine enthusiasm for the fulfillment of our goal to make cymatic therapy available to people in the United States. When we first met, we were trying to overcome the at-odds relationship between a short, proper British osteopath, who hadn't the patience for inquiries, and a tall, spirited American woman with no traditional medical degrees, but who had a lot of questions. We found ourselves in a situation that required an amazing amount of trust—not to mention faith—in a new paradigm of healing.

Since my initial results with friends and family were so successful, it wasn't long before I called Dr. Manners and invited him to visit me in the states. In September 2001, we needed to begin discussions on how to create a completely new device. Fortunately, I already knew some factory owners who could potentially collaborate with me on the manufacturing.

However, in my phone call with Dr. Manners he said he would have to bring his bodyguard. In my previous visits, I had never seen a bodyguard at his clinic or when we were together in public. I also never saw any evidence of British police protection. I wondered, since he was traveling outside of the country, if there were any new threats that caused him to feel he needed protection in the United States. Regardless, I willingly bought two tickets.

When Dr. Manners and his bodyguard arrived, they were transporting two more of the exact same devices I had previously purchased. We had arranged to meet in the dining room of a hotel, and I was relieved to see Dr. Manners looking well. Comically, next to his small frame came the bodyguard, who was overly muscular and at least six feet tall. He wore a suit, tie, and sunglasses—resembling a questionable character right out of a 1940s film noir. When Dr. Manners introduced him, he had a very identifiably Italian name. He worked security at large music concerts throughout Europe and, according to him, had been a bodyguard for Sting. So why was he protecting Dr. Manners…?

Later, we joined our manufacturing collaborators in a small conference room. They had invited a friend with a shoulder problem to meet with us, so Dr. Manners could demonstrate how the device worked. We stood around the chair the client was sitting in, with great anticipation, to see what his response would be to the treatment. Would he say his shoulder felt better after one session?

After a few moments of the sound being applied to his shoulder, the subject reported he didn't feel anything. This was actually not unusual after the first application. What concerned me more was the look on Dr. Manners' face. He appeared to be listening intently to the hum of the frequencies.

"There must be something wrong," he said. He continued, greatly disturbed, "These don't sound like the correct frequencies."

My technical team from the West Coast offered to take a look at the device, to see if they could figure out what the problem was. Dr. Manners willingly stepped aside saying, "Please, do have a look."

When they opened the unit from the back and peered in, there was a note from the British assembler. It said that some of the elements had been disconnected, so as not to be fully operable.

Apparently, he had heard that Dr. Manners was considering another business partner in the States and had decided to ruin his plan. Even though my technical team could see that Dr. Manners had been sabotaged, they were less than kind in their description of what they were viewing. Not helping was that it didn't look like a healing instrument you would find in a medical office.

"This is just a simple frequency generator! This is no 'special sound-healing device' at all," the first man exclaimed.

"I saw things like this when I was in the military," the other man added. "Where did these parts come from—off the shelf of some outdated supply house?"

They both turned to me shaking their heads in disbelief. Then one of them spoke, "You've been taken."

I saw the whole scenario explode before my eyes. I felt myself in a hurricane of questions. My faith in it all was being tested to the extreme.

Dr. Manners looked tremendously embarrassed and completely dejected. He turned away and walked out of the room with his head down, refusing to look at me. He didn't even attempt to make eye contact. Was he acting this way because he had been found out?

In a few brief moments, my team totally dismissed the device and the therapy. My dream was shattered; the deal was off. I had a device that I knew worked, but no one would believe me now. If he had tried to explain the situation or apologize for the scene we had just witnessed, I might have remained steady despite the disastrous proceedings that were unfolding before me. Why wasn't he standing here with me to defend it?

I had trusted Dr. Manners to demonstrate the incredible results the instrument could produce. Instead, he failed in front of us all. Perhaps he was just *using* this therapy; he certainly hadn't *made* the device. After all, shouldn't he have had some knowledge of the inner workings of the instrument after applying and researching it for the last forty years?

As it turned out, the bodyguard knew the assembler personally and offered to call him. Would Dr. Manners' protector turn out to be the one to rescue the situation—despite my initial misgivings?

In the hallway, he and Dr. Manners initiated a three-way transatlantic phone call with the assembler. While talking over a speakerphone with raised voices and accusatory tones, they described to him what had happened. The two of them demanded that he disclose how he had made the instrument inoperable. My team and I were eavesdropping in the conference room, and they continued to poke fun at the device. Over the phone, outside in the hallway, the assembler was laughing and saying, "The rigging was just a little joke!" Then Dr. Manners demanded that he explain how it had been made inoperable. After much arguing, he grudgingly gave them the instructions to unlock the device.

The two of them came running back into the room, explaining they knew how to make it work. One of my team members took their instructions and simply flipped a hidden switch, and though Dr. Manners seemed to think it was repaired, my team members had already dismissed the effectiveness of the device. The damage had been done. The situation had disintegrated to the point that the team no longer wanted to be involved, and to my extreme frustration, they left the room with smirks on their faces.

I knew Dr. Manners realized that the deal was unraveling, and I needed time to process what had transpired. With intense frustration and deep disappointment I said to them, "Tonight, I think we should all have dinner alone."

Sadly, they turned and walked out of the room without responding.

Later that night I saw them in the lobby, and I announced that the trip was over. I told them I would make arrangements for them to leave on a flight the next day. They did not try to change my mind, and we parted ways.

I was back to rehashing my doubts with no path forward. I was sure the device worked, because I had seen the proof with Dr. Manners' patients and with my own clients as well. But my plans would be on hold until I could figure out how to create a new device, if indeed there was still a reason to make one. And I knew I couldn't do this alone.

Looking back now, I have come to understand the twists and turns of fate that were affecting the destiny of this new therapy. Dr. Manners' connecting flight was on September 10, from the JFK Airport. He left with many of my questions unanswered. The next day was September 11, when the terrorist acts and their ensuing devastation took place in our country. Fortunately, Dr. Manners made it home safely before the plane crashes. If he had stayed one more day, as originally planned, he would have been flying out of New York in the midst of the chaos.

After the unfavorable encounter we had, he was forced to deal with the problems he was having in the United Kingdom in order to continue his current manufacturing. As far as I was concerned, he would have to assure me there would be no further problems should we start our discussions again. Additional proof would be needed regarding his therapy, his device, and its origins. Personally, I was barely holding on; every aspect of my world had been turned upside down. I was perplexed as to what my next step should be.

Within a week, Dr. Manners called me to apologize, but at this point, too many doubts had been raised. I was very cool at the beginning of the conversation. I demanded that he be forthcoming about his techniques, his patients' records, and how his therapy really worked. He had to have sensed my frustration and how my enthusiasm had waned.

Then he said, "I am sorry. Please allow me to come back. I will give you all the information you are asking for."

My heart was listening, but my mind was doubting. Still, I agreed we should meet again. When he returned to the United States that October (sans bodyguard), he brought a heavy, dark-brown cardboard folder packed with loose-leaf papers. I was full of anticipation as I opened it, not sure what to expect. To my surprise and elation, there was page after page of grids filled with cymatic codes. Each one represented a specific pattern consisting of five frequencies.

The entries included a description of which body system it supported. Not only did it contain frequencies that addressed the human form but *also* the energy body that is so often referred to in Chinese medicine and the ancient texts of Ayurveda. With this realization, I knew I could take Dr. Manners' work to a new level of understanding.

This folder of information was stunning in its implication: there must be some algorithm or geometric correlation that made sound healing possible. In my mind, I could see three-dimensional forms, five-sided figures, and pentagonal shapes floating in their own spheres. I was beginning to realize I held the secrets that could create infinite possibilities of sound healing. In that moment, all the doubts and difficulties Dr. Manners and I had been through left me. I could see the miracle of it all.

Besides this folder, he promised to be forthcoming with a lot more information from his patient files, which would also help validate his therapy. I wanted to believe he was a professional who would be able to share lots of information on the healing of his patients. However, at the same time, he was using archaic sound therapy devices to treat them. He acknowledged he had neither designed nor built them, and that he had no engineering background.

The members of the original group of scientists he worked with were now impossible to find. There was no schematic for building the old devices, or any reason to continue with this outdated design. In our conversations, he became increasingly excited about the prospect of my ideas for a whole new device. By early December, we had created our first business contract regarding my use of the body of work he had presented to me.

Later that month, I returned to the clinic with the idea I would review his patients' files. I was looking for success stories I could share with others in the States. I found some notes regarding patients written by Dr. Manners and other staff members, but unfortunately, for the most part, I was disappointed to find these observations were incomplete. There were little to no written accounts of the successes that had been achieved.

There were standard medical intake forms and notes for the first three or four visits, then nothing. When I questioned Dr. Manners about this, he always said the patients had gotten well and needed no further treatment. He dismissed my concerns and declared many cases had resolved quickly. However, most of what I saw in the documents wouldn't be considered acceptable record keeping or reliable information by the standards of American doctors.

In February 2002, I had begun to assemble a team consisting of marketers, promoters, and educators. Also, the small manufacturing company I had established a relationship with was willing to work with me to create a whole new device. After coining the term *Cymatherapy*, I established the company Cymatherapy International to oversee all aspects of production, distribution, and training.

But now, since I was returning home with less than definitive answers, I decided not to share the unacceptable record keeping I had found with my team. They were already busy creating a plan to manufacture the next evolution of a sound therapy device. Besides, in no way were they looking to replicate the old one. I was totally invested in bringing forth a new device that would work consistently and reliably, while utilizing the same healing principles and original frequencies that I had promised Dr. Manners to protect.

It was clear to me that as soon as the manufacturing was complete, I would need my own research to prove the mathematics and the science behind the efficacy of this form of healing. I needed to bring all the concepts together to support his body of work.

Meanwhile, I had stopped offering treatment to people in order to focus my efforts. During this time, I was fortunate to meet a medical nurse named Liz Colorio who had been involved in alternative healthcare research. She was working in an orthopedic clinic in Massachusetts. She agreed to come to Atlanta to learn about the device. She also requested permission to use it with patients she was working with. I gave her my personal device for this important research.

I remembered Dr. Manners had told us that his original group of collaborators had early success with treating pain and inflammation, and as soon as Liz's results started coming in, we could see that, most assuredly, cymatic therapy was working in these areas. I went back to my business partners with this proof.

Throughout my time of expansive learning with Dr. Manners, I continued to search for other scientists, healers, and researchers who were working with sound. There were very few people who knew about cymatic therapy or who had any understanding of how it worked. I continued to struggle with whether I should tell everyone I knew about it or not. What if the healing sessions I had witnessed were not replicable for everyone?

Fortunately, I knew other alternative medicine healers. I spent time introducing Dr. Manners' work to them, to see if other therapies could work in conjunction with his. One of these people was Margaret Ruby. She had a large following on the West Coast and in the United Kingdom. She was able to bring to the forefront her esoteric view of cymatic therapy. This was important because I wanted to make sure emotional components and esoteric teachings were included in the study and practice of sound therapy.

During this time, one of Margaret's students by the name of Annaliese became interested in helping me. She felt called to learn more about sound therapy and would become one of the first Cymatherapy practitioners and a wonderful teacher. She joined me some months later in the important quest to train other practitioners.

When our manufacturing team was finished producing the first device, I named it the Cyma 1000. As previously related, in early 2002, I had coined the term Cymatherapy. It gave recognition to Dr. Manners' original title of "cymatic therapy," but also pointed to the American evolution of a new device and the new manufacturing techniques employed. A couple years later, as I planned the unveiling of the Cyma 1000, I called Dr. Manners with a personal invitation to come to the United States to share in this special event. At the time, he was approaching his 101st birthday and was unable to join us, but he expressed his excitement about a future unveiling in the United Kingdom.

It was January 2005, and I was ready to introduce the Cyma 1000 to the world. In an Atlanta hotel ballroom, I unveiled the new instrument. It was met with great excitement by my friends, fellow practitioners, associates, and business partners. I was elated. People came from all over the world to see it. After what had felt like an eternity, this spectacular dream had come true!

Chapter Five

The Wild Card

In 2004, while working to perfect the Cyma 1000 prototype and searching for other research partners and visionaries who would help me spread the word about sound therapy, I encountered people who were just as passionate about helping animals as I was about helping humans. I was introduced to many caring individuals, both doctors and practitioners, who were extraordinary healers in the veterinary field. Some of my best examples of how Cymatherapy works on injuries came from the competitive world of horse racing.

It was during this time my first website was constructed to announce the release of the Cyma 1000 in the United States. Via this site, I connected with an equine massage therapist. She knew about sound therapy, worked with numerous horses and several veterinarians, and introduced me to a doctor who was using acupuncture on race horses. He was also open to the use of sound therapy.

Interestingly enough, when Dr. Manners presented me with the list of codes, included were very specific frequencies for the equine population. He never explained to me why those codes were on the list. Since he neither owned any horses, nor ever administered therapy to any in my presence, it remains a mystery. All I know is I have seen the codes work repeatedly, providing a level of healing almost beyond imagination.

I learned quickly that race horses are athletes; when they are injured, it can mean the end of their careers—if not their lives. They are often viewed as no longer valuable if they are not competing. So, with the help of the vet and the massage therapist, I was given the opportunity to create a research model to show how quickly sound could repair torn tendons.

We decided to work on this area since it was a common injury in horses. When damaged, it wasn't unusual to see a 25–35% tear in their leg tendons (which resemble Achilles tendons in humans). We created an initial protocol we thought would be most effective. We'd administer Cymatherapy for twenty-minute sessions directly on the horse's injured leg, applying the sound five times a week for the first two weeks, followed by three times a week for four weeks. With diagnostic ultrasound, we captured images every ten days to monitor any improvements in the injured tissue.

We also received important feedback through the horses' body language. We would often observe them shifting their weight to get comfortable for the session, or moving closer to us to receive the sound. The horses' ears would lay back and their eyes would begin to close, as if relaxing or preparing to take a nap. These responses were exhibited by all the horses who experienced the therapy.

After ten sessions, the vet came by to see how things were going. The initial scans indicated progress—showing the tendon tissue repairing. We decided to continue the therapy, with the vet's oversight and a review every ten days. To everyone's surprise, at the end of the six week study, the torn tissue was totally regenerated. The doctor couldn't believe his eyes. There was a feeling of great celebration among us. The study gave hope to owners of horses who believed they had no other choice but to abandon them after this kind of injury.

Then came the real test. A powerfully beautiful animal named The Frac, who was perfectly bred and destined for greatness, was in the middle of a race when he stepped in a hole and had to be ambulanced off the track. His owner was devastated. Everyone watching felt sure that the animal's racing career was over. As usual, it was recommended to the owner the horse be put down. However, our equine therapist knew this gentleman and arranged for the horse to have access to our six week protocol.

Again, through diagnostic ultrasound, we tracked the horse from the time of injury throughout the protocol, and there was an incredible healing of a 95% tear of his tendon. The Frac's case netted some of my most profound images. They provided proof that Cymatherapy healed a condition that had been considered impossible to repair. The healing was so complete that the tissue looked like it had never been injured.

Not to mention, the horse became eligible to race again and actually won! This created quite a buzz amongst the members of the gaming commission. But no illegal drugs, or other wrong doing, could be found in connection with this horse; only sound therapy was used to resurrect his life and career.

I continue to show these images in my public presentations, and through them I have encouraged many who were skeptical to take a second look at Cymatherapy. I'd also like to acknowledge that many times research itself negatively impacts the health and well-being of animals. In this case, I knew our research might actually save the horse's racing career, let alone his life. At no time did we cause him additional pain or discomfort. In fact, we hastened his recovery, lessened his pain, and got him back on the track sooner.

It's plain that race horses, like other athletes, suffer from the chronic use and abuse of their bodies, especially during the height of their careers. But we forget these animals also suffer from anxiety, due in part to the demands that humans place on them during competitive racing.

Because of the scrutiny of the gaming commission, no drug or any substance can be used to calm the horse or enhance his performance before a race.

While the equine codes Dr. Manners provided for me didn't include emotional-balancing frequencies for horses, we found the relaxation codes created for humans were helpful to animals as well. In fact, when many of the owners saw how successful we were at helping their animals, they became interested in experiencing Cymatherapy too.

I am so grateful to the veterinarians, trainers, and equine massage practitioners who have been willing to adopt the use of my device in their respective fields. I truly believe there will be much less drug-related animal abuse as sound therapy becomes more accepted. I am happy to see Cymatherapy being integrated into other complementary and alternative medical strategies that are developing for animals, as well as humans, in a profoundly compassionate way.

These experiences underscored the need to get this information out to a world in desperate need of it. How could I move this process along more quickly? The potential to alleviate suffering in both humans and animals was so great, I couldn't stop thinking about it. I realized that those waking up to the idea of energy medicine needed like-minded people to work and share knowledge with. It occurred to me, emerging voices in science and vibrational medicine needed a forum—a place to put forth new ideas. Perhaps I could create such an opportunity.

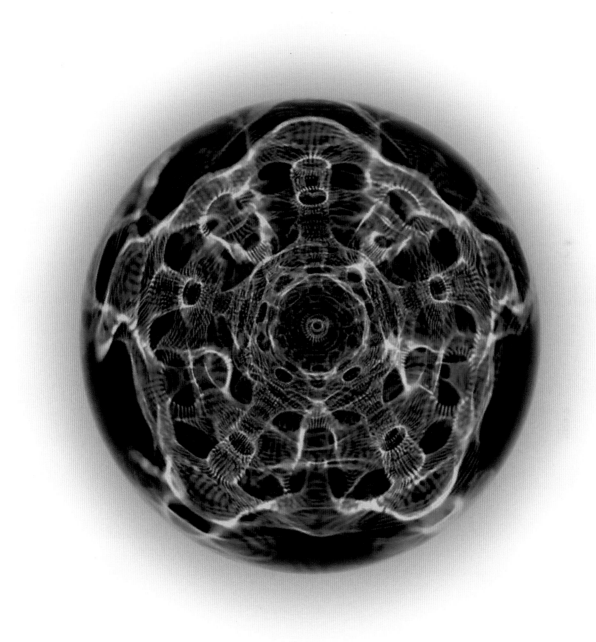

Chapter Six

Organizing Chaos

In line with my inspiration regarding some sort of forum to exchange new ideas, during one of my meditations in 2005, I heard a voice telling me I should create a sound therapy association. I envisioned it would enlist international members, and it would influence many to try therapeutic sound. I knew people around the world were starting to recognize its healing power, and I wanted to connect the new voices in the field. Creating a community of healers who would be open to working with the Cyma 1000 device was also part of my mission. It had been four years since I had originally met Dr. Manners, and with this new goal, I realized my work with Cymatherapy was just beginning.

Jeff Volk (who had organized *The International Sound Colloquium* years before and was one of the first people to explore the sound-healing arena beyond the use of music) was a source of inspiration and very helpful in creating this new community by drawing together many people from the worlds of sound and music. And so, after discussions with friends and other like-minded associates, the International Sound Therapy Association (ISTA) almost created itself. With ISTA, I wanted to honor the ancient traditions of sacred sound, which I felt very connected to from my life's experiences, but I also wanted to represent modern day therapeutic sound by shining a light on new discoveries in the field.

Many people were getting excited about my Cymatherapy device, so I was focusing on how the technical aspect could become relevant in the future of sound therapy. In this current age, everyone wants more convenient therapies with faster results. People are hoping for healing treatments that address all aspects of the human being simultaneously.

I have read and heard so many stories of cultures that sing souls back together. The tribes use their particular sound as a remembrance—a means of entrainment—to reconnect their members, especially if there are problems or illnesses among them. In the same way, yoga teachings help us remember our higher selves through mantras. Other forms of sound or music, like "Ava Maria," invoke the divine feminine within each of us and call us back to our collective selves.

In ancient times, adepts spent years becoming clear channels, preparing themselves so that healing could be transmitted effectively. The expectation was that the healer as a channel was pure. Modern day practitioners need instruction, proficiency, and the tools to help them create this pure intention.

In this day and time, playing the ancient instruments can be a so-called cool thing to do. Without training, this can result in participants not receiving the effect they were looking for, with responses they don't understand. Some individuals are born with a valuable gift of intuition. This can be a great complement to an established body of knowledge that practitioners have taken the time to study. All instruments have their respective range of frequencies that produce their own set of therapeutic effects. We must remember: not all sound is good for everyone, and all therapies are not appropriate for everybody.

Every honored profession, every lineage, has a progression of learning and mastery. People have been playing ancient instruments for hundreds of years. I wanted to bring these sound techniques into the 21st century and have them recognized as a viable tool for helping to heal humanity. If a student was attending medical school, they would begin by learning established knowledge and techniques. This would be practiced for a length of time, until proficiency was reached. What would follow is a level of mastery that could include an awareness, or a series of intuitive hunches, about what the client or patient might need for their healing.

Viewing the current state of the accepted medical system, I believed sound therapy had to become an important aspect of the new vibrational or energy medicine. With all its incredible potential, I envisioned sound as the perfect remedy for a world needing to be called back into harmony. However, sound therapy needed to be taught correctly in order to be utilized as a viable tool. ISTA could provide education in ancient and modern sound techniques and be the vehicle to collect knowledge and research on both, which then could be shared.

When Jeff heard that the organization was in operation, he told me about the British acoustics engineer John Stuart Reid and his work to make sound visible. He was following in the steps of predecessors like Hans Jenny to create what he called a CymaScope. John had also met Dr. Manners, but only for a brief period, and he was very excited to hear about my new developments with the Cyma 1000. Serendipitously, he was scheduled to come to the United States in April of 2005, and Jeff arranged for us to meet.

During my first conversation with John, we spoke excitedly about the potential of making Dr. Manners' frequency research visible with his CymaScope and the Cyma 1000. I was thrilled at the thought of seeing sound images created by my new device. At the time of our get-together, plans were also forming for the unveiling of the Cyma 1000 in the United Kingdom. Since Annaliese was considering traveling on the UK tour with me, I had invited her to attend the meeting with John. She knew many international students who had studied with Margaret Ruby, and we were both excited about the prospect of introducing them to Cymatherapy.

During this meeting, John graciously invited us both to visit his laboratory and to host the first Cymatherapy training-weekend for participants in the United Kingdom. I couldn't have been happier! This meant we would witness the sounds of the Cyma 1000 in dynamic patterns with his CymaScope, but it also meant I would have to choose what I felt were the most important first images to view from 750 different commutations (or code combinations). After many hours of consideration, I finally decided to begin with some of the subtle body commutations. I was curious about how sound impacts the interface of the physical and the subtle bodies.

The specific code that reflects the energy of the etheric body held great fascination for me. From my studies, I concluded that our physical forms are energetically infused from our subtle bodies. The etheric sheath is the energy field closest to the physical form, and I wondered which cymatic shapes would strengthen it and what they might look like. I also believed the particular etheric body held the keys for vibrant health.

Back then, John was trying to perfect the techniques used by his early predecessors. We weren't really sure what we would be able to see. As with any early experimentation, there were many elements to control. When bringing new concepts to light, few people realize the difficult obstacles to overcome and the multiple challenges to be met.

Everyone who attended the training was invited into John's laboratory to witness the first attempts to see the healing sounds. All who observed the sound pattern unfolding were in awe of the visuals before us. This was the very first cymatic experiment based upon sounds coming from the Cyma 1000. It was the beginning of making the 750 codes visible in our time. No one, anywhere, had ever seen images of this particular frequency before. Even John was astonished!

We all stood around the CymaScope in wonderment, overwhelmed by the staggering possibilities of what might come and what this could mean for sound therapy as a whole. I was mesmerized by the dancing salt particles, and I attempted to comprehend it all. At the same time, I was having a kinesthetic experience watching the visual of the sound vibration of the etheric body. I had a deep recognition of it.

In celebration of all that had happened, John, Annaliese, and I decided to travel to Scotland to visit the Roslyn Chapel, known for its mystical history since the 1500s. During the drive, we discussed the Cymatherapy training and the continuation of it in the United Kingdom. As we spoke about the development of cymatics and future endeavors, I noticed that there was another kind of excitement building—I was watching the remarkable love affair between John and Annaliese begin to unfold.

After our visit to the United Kingdom, they were inseparable. In their life together, they worked diligently to promote the research of sound therapy and its efficacy as a healing modality. They became instrumental in introducing the world to visible sound with the exquisite images John created using the CymaScope.

As I revisit my memory of the original cymatic image John created in salt, I remember thinking that it was the most incredible thing I had ever seen. Yet nothing compares to the dynamic images of the cymatic codes he brings forth today, with his own invention and new technology.

In 2017, he released this statement:

"Sound patterns created by the CymaScope are called 'CymaGlyphs' and are literally the geometry of sound made visible. The perfection of these beautiful patterns of sound often give the impression of being computer generated, when they are actually a natural manifestation of sound's vibrations imprinting on the surface and subsurface of pure water or other fluids. Whenever sound is present CymaGlyph patterns occur all around us and even within us, as it imprints on the trillions of water rich cellular membranes that make up the body. The interaction of sound on cellular membranes has triggered the emergence of it as a powerful healing modality."

For me, John has been an authoritative voice in acoustic science. I have always cherished our discussions on theories of how sound effects cells, and the vision sharing with both he and Annaliese. He has been brilliant in showing me that when a *sound flower* appears on the surface of the water, there is also a phasing going on in the depths—another flower is unfolding underneath. His work has made me aware of this exquisite expression of natural beauty, which signals the unending progression of nature.

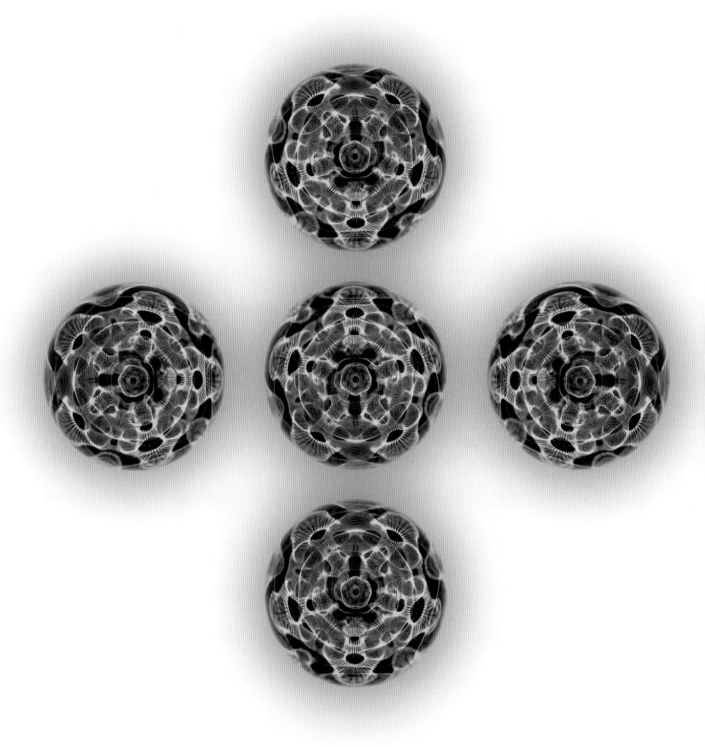

Chapter Seven

The Physician and the Metaphysician

*T*he 2005 trip to the United Kingdom was incredibly successful. My only sadness occurred at not being able to introduce the device at the Bretforton Clinic. Dr. Manners had decided, earlier that year, to retire and close his facility. He was impressed with the new Cyma 1000 when he saw it, and he knew that this device would insure his life's work would continue. Unfortunately, after his long years of service and the closing of this chapter of his life, we had less contact.

Even sadder, following his retirement he started experiencing the early stages of dementia. I reflected on the first time I met him and how vibrant, agile, and quick-witted he was—even at age 97. From the beginning, I observed that cyma frequencies may have had aspects that created a fountain-of-youth effect in the body. So, when he was no longer immersed in his work with them, his health began to deteriorate.

In some ways, the Bretforton Clinic was a type of Shangri-La, hidden away in a small village, where people regained their health easily with the simple, targeted approach of his cymatic therapy. As far as life there, it was like nothing ever changed; I was envious of the ease with which Dr. Manners had been able to live. He cared for many people while retaining his own vibrancy.

The last time I called him, I invited him to the United States. Sadly, he declined. He left me with these words, "No, my work is done. It's your turn now."

The teacher was telling the student, "It's time for you to go forth on your own."

This made me realize—at some point, we must pass the baton. Sometimes we need to graduate into a leadership position, whether we feel ready or not. I anticipated this transition; yet, I thought I would have him for a few more years. This reminded me of the day I left the ashram to take Baba's teachings into the outside world. I was released then too, to blossom on my own.

Even with freedom, there was still fear. Had Dr. Manners given me all the necessary information? Was there more truth, more knowledge, he could have imparted to me? Regardless of my doubts, I had strong personal convictions on my side, let alone the urging of an angelic being. I believed this had been handed to me as my destiny. I have always tried to honor Dr. Manners and have striven to respect his life's work. It was important to me that he'd be happy with how the rest of the story unfolded.

With the handing over of the torch, I'll also admit I felt a sense of relief. I needed room for my own vision to shine. I wanted to take cymatic therapy out of the small clinic in Bretforton and bring Cymatherapy to a larger worldwide arena.

I knew there would be a lot more research required and solid scientific reinforcement of the principles of this new field of energy medicine. I hadn't been sure Dr. Manners was the person to provide convincing arguments to the world we live in. There were plenty of circumstances where he wouldn't have been the right messenger, especially to those who were extremely skeptical or those demanding proof of every statement he made.

I believe a special mantle comes over an individual when they are living their true purpose. Each day, it is a challenge to stay out of the ego state and choose the correct path to serve humanity. I knew there would be new devices to create, new applications for the therapy, and further development of his commutations.

After a period of time, truly feeling the loss of his presence, I realized I had everything I needed. My spiritual connection to the divine principles deep within my heart, and the faith I felt that any challenges could be overcome, helped me to stabilize. I maintained my optimistic view that the world can evolve, even if the full vision hasn't been understood yet. Much had been given to me to move sound healing forward, and I believed my Cymatherapy devices would be prominent in a new type of medicine chest for people everywhere to use.

Since my first visit with Dr. Manners—up through and beyond his passing in 2009— there have been great developments in the science of Cymatherapy. When I think back to the successes he was having at the Bretforton Clinic, I can only imagine what he would say now, seeing the healing power of sound accessed all over the world—with the utilization of his research and the new Cymatherapy devices available to many.

Every day I read something new on the internet about "frequency." There are many different approaches and schools of thought regarding sound and energy medicine. I enjoy watching the new field emerge with all of its possibilities, but I continue to search for the highest truths and proven concepts in it all.

Of special interest to me is the use of frequency to imprint various substances. In my first visit to Dr. Manners, I experienced the swimming pool—full of healing frequencies. I have always been fascinated by the way water carries information, because water is a superb conductor of sound (sound travels 4–6 times faster through it). In fact, our bodies are over 70% water.

Many sound practitioners have shared with me how they imprint the specific Cyma healing frequencies into glass containers of water. This is done by simply placing a light-weight receptacle on the device and choosing the channel that your body most needs. Playing the frequency into the water allows it to be charged or imprinted with sounds your cells recognize. Your body absorbs the information while you are drinking it.

Some practitioners charge the water with codes used in a session, to further extend the healing process after the session is over. This is not to be confused with homeopathy, which is a well-known and accepted form of energy medicine. Both techniques follow similar trains of thought. Homeopathy, by definition, treats disease with minute doses of natural substances that follow the premise of "like cures like." These substances are tinctures made with water that are designed to elicit a certain response in the body for fighting disease.

With my devices, the sound message is imprinted on the cells, the visceral waters of the body, or the water you drink. These are frequencies the body recognizes, to repair it or prepare it for a fight against disease.

Imprinting with sound occurs whether it is the sounds in the environment, the voices of others, or the repetitive nature of our own thoughts. I believe the frequencies are a pure message, untainted by less-than-positive thoughts or unclear intentions. Spiritual teachings have long cautioned us about the power of our words and our thoughts, and how they impact our surroundings and the world as a whole. The energetic codes help to shore up the vital body so neither inner nor outer influences are likely to have a negative effect.

Dr. Manners disclosed to me that he worked with a collaborative group of researchers during a time when the first realizations about what sound healing could do were being considered. My last ten years have been devoted to researching ways to most successfully utilize these codes, producing astounding results. The findings of researchers, the expertise of engineers, and the experiences of practitioners have shown me how to evolve Dr. Manners' efforts into highly effective protocols and the development of future channels. The most successful ones I have created to date are named the Cyma Ten.

All of Dr. Manners work is utilized in the Cyma Ten and also in the development of future channels. His codes are being combined in new ways to address the various health challenges of the client that require attention if healing is to be complete. I have gathered this information through years of study, as well as from the knowledge shared with me by many other experts in various fields.

Dr. Manners accepted many esoteric forms of healing, and he insisted a certain amount of traditional medicine be included in his approach to Cymatherapy as well. However, had I not come to Bretforton, his approach to the therapy might never have evolved, and his knowledge may never have passed beyond the borders of his small town. I believe he was an important messenger who introduced this information to us. We must continue to develop it in order to fully understand how it is to be used, both now and in the future.

Chapter Eight

The Light of Science

*B*etween the years of 2001 and 2003, I continued my consulting business, using it as a vehicle to introduce the idea of the Cyma 1000 to healthcare practitioners. This often evolved into collaborations with like-minded holistic professionals who wanted to understand how Cymatherapy could be integrated into their practices. One of them was a doctor with an integrative medical practice in Atlanta who had installed a thermography camera in his office. He brought in a specialized technician periodically to provide thermal imaging for his patients.

Prior to this, when I had attended a health conference in Florida in 1997, I'd been introduced to thermography as an important tool for detecting and monitoring changes in tissue. In fact, in some cases, it showed cellular change years before it would appear on other more traditional forms of testing. In my studies, I also learned it was capable of showing other changes in the body.

Since we had consulted on other cases, this doctor was open to hearing about my new device. He also offered to assist me in gathering more information. One of my greatest challenges had indeed been proving how the therapy worked without access to tests like MRI or CAT scans. Thermography could serve that purpose and was an obvious choice. Now I had this contact. First though, he was interested in having his own sound session to have a fuller understanding of it, before offering it to his patients.

Since he had no specific health problems at the time, we provided him with our stress relief protocol. He experienced a thirty-minute session lying on a massage table while one of the recent graduates of our Cymatherapy training provided the therapy. After his session, he reported he had not experienced such a deep level of relaxation since before he had started medical school and embarked on his career. He was so impressed he invited the practitioner to continue offering the therapy at his office.

Fortunately, he understood the importance of helping people de-stress and the implication it can have on promoting good health and the prevention of disease. He was also reading the medical journals of the time that were beginning to identify stress as the underlying cause of many serious illnesses

Soon after, I approached him with a proposal to use the thermal imaging at his office to investigate the efficacy of Cymatherapy on improving the circulatory system. Because of his confidence in me and this new therapy, he was willing to invite his patients to participate in this preliminary study.

We assembled a team which included the doctor as overseeing physician, Liz (the RN we had previously worked with), a Cymatherapy practitioner, and myself. With the doctor's permission, we were able to review the patients' health histories. While an earlier study of mine in the United States had been with horses, this research in Atlanta would be my chance to show proof with human beings.

Even though I had previously learned a lot about thermal imaging and how it worked, I still needed someone who could explain to me what I was viewing. They, in turn, had to have an understanding about Cymatherapy, to look for indications it might or might not be working. Also, I realized that each of the 750 commutations needed to be tested for their efficacy.

We were attempting to find out if specific Cymatherapy codes could increase circulation. We were interested in this, in part, because of the importance of bringing oxygen-rich blood to the cells. Also, it was a fairly simple test to run with the thermal imaging device. The first step was to determine if there was a lack of circulation in the ten clients who enrolled in the study.

First, the forearms of the clients were scanned. Then we administered the Cyma codes designated to increase circulation. We wanted to see if the thermographic images indicated a change. Every single client showed an increase in vascular activity in their limbs. I have been asked why we decided to do the test on the forearm. Unlike x-ray or MRI, thermography can only penetrate one-half to three-quarter inches into the body. With this first project, we were only looking for the ability to affect change in vascular activity. Following the study, the participants happily continued Cymatherapy, alongside their regular medical care. With increased circulation, they were assured a greater potential for better health.

As simple as the previous study may sound, it led me to the extremely important research to follow. It became increasingly clear that not only would I need to prove the efficacy of the therapy, code by code, but more research would also be required on how the codes worked in pairs and in groups—in order to ensure the ultimate use of the therapy and the device I had created. Working alone on future studies looked to be a long slow path to discover what I already knew could work.

What I needed was a dedicated individual who was willing to conduct ongoing research. Fortunately, Liz was interested in continuing the process. The knowledge she gained from the Atlanta study, along with her data gathered in Massachusetts, inspired her to look deeper into the possibilities of what this therapy could do for circulation and pain.

She had a brilliant colleague, Dr. Anthony Fleming, a mathematical physicist and biophysicist, who was extremely interested in our preliminary findings. He was also the founder of the Biophotonics Research Institute in Australia. We shared the thermal imaging findings and case studies with him. With his expertise in science and math, combined with Liz's medical research experience, they were able author a paper they were both extraordinarily excited about. They planned to submit it to the BEMS (Bioelectromagnetic Society), an international organization of professionals, which promotes the exchange of ideas to advance the science of natural and applied electromagnetic fields in biology and medicine. Dr. Fleming was a member of this society and felt the group would be interested in the findings.

In 2007, the paper was accepted. Dr. Fleming presented our groundbreaking research to his colleagues at the BEMS where it was widely praised. Further research was encouraged by the society, which resulted in an invitation to return for a more in-depth presentation in 2008.

I was elated! Finally, there was some validation.

The one thing I have always known about this therapy and my devices is that they operate with *acoustic sound*, which has no known side effects. But still, from the beginning of my journey, there has been a constant barrage of questions. How do you know it works? Why doesn't my doctor know about this? Where is the research? Any attempts I made to explain were met with skepticism and doubt. Whereas, many healing techniques used successfully by doctors and alternative healthcare practitioners have not been proven by science. In many cases, drugs are released to the public with far less research than I have been asked to provide. I knew if I waited until every single code and premise had been validated, I wouldn't see the therapy made available, in this lifetime, to those who desperately need it.

My research using thermal imaging has produced some of the most astounding healing images ever seen. They prove a decrease in inflammation and an increase of circulation, both of which are extremely important in alleviating pain. Thermography also produces no known side effects. The visuals simply reinforce the thousands of testimonials I have received. Even before this proof, I had an innate knowingness that Cymatherapy worked. I believe the body possesses a divine intelligence and utilizes sound as a cell-to-cell communication system. Put simply, the vibrations of the healing frequencies call the cells back into harmony.

Each person's story reminds me of the difference sound can make in one's health and quality of life. While I continue to prove this premise with modern diagnostic assessment tools, I still take the greatest comfort in knowing what I hold in my heart to be true.

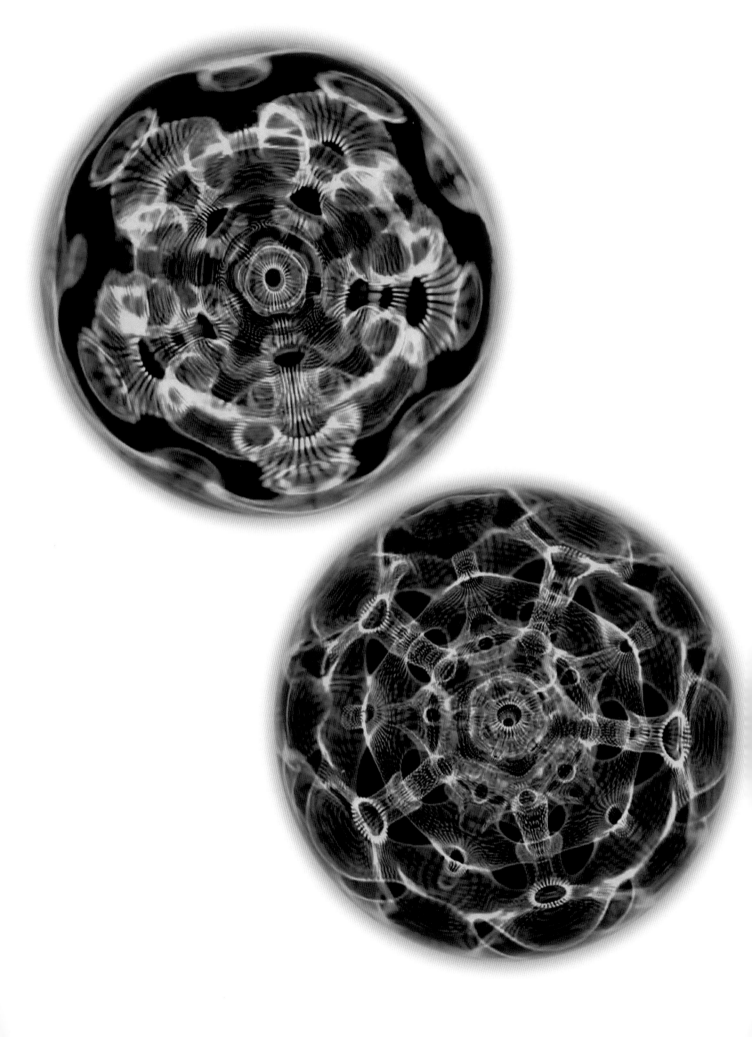

Chapter Nine

Gifts From Lord Shiva

From the beginning, I saw Cymatherapy as the medicine of the future. The CymaScope had showed us the dynamic action sound can have on every cell, and the BEMS had lauded our research with great praise. Meanwhile, during this period of exciting exploration, Jeff Volk continued to connect me with other sound innovators, including a man in Germany by the name of Alexander Lauterwasser. Jeff had published an English translation of his beautiful book entitled *Water Sound Images*, which I first enjoyed in 2007. Through Jeff, I received an invitation to visit Alexander's laboratory. I flew to Germany later that year to explore his perspective on sound.

While most of the early sound images had been created in powder, the ones created in water had a very special dynamic quality. To me, they looked more alive. Since our bodies are over 70% water, I was thrilled with the idea of imprinting sound at a cellular level. During my visit, I learned that he was a photographer and a practicing psychologist. He came from a family of acclaimed photographers, whose artistry he had clearly inherited. His own talent was exhibited beautifully in *Water Sound Images*.

He had a genuine appreciation for the natural beauty of tortoises. His love for the intricate design of their shells was reflected in his photographs of cymatic images. As I looked at them, I remembered the story of the legendary Chinese Emperor Fu Shi. While contemplating upon the shell of a tortoise, he experienced the realization of the I Ching.

My first meeting with Alexander was scheduled nearby in a small town in Switzerland. It was to take place before a music concert he was participating in. He was planning to capture the visual images generated by the sound of the musicians in the concert, and upon my arrival at the venue, he was unloading a van full of equipment. We greeted each other briefly, and as the music started (an improvisational piece by a flutist and a percussionist), the first images on the screen—created in real time—were miraculous. The music was dynamic, which caused the images to pulse and dance; they reflected an amazing light. Personally, I felt deeply relaxed while listening and watching. The rest of the audience (a small group of about forty people) were captivated by the combination of visuals and sound.

I imagined how music enthusiasts in the United States would have enjoyed it. I wished more people from all over the world could have experienced this spectacular event. After an enlightening performance, we spoke briefly to schedule a meeting at his laboratory the next morning. I returned to the hotel full of hope and excitement.

During our getting-to-know-each-other conversation the following day, a curious coincidence came to light. He described the music lessons he had taken as a young man, which was when he first started experimenting with sound. His teacher suggested he should meet Hans Jenny, a medical doctor and a natural scientist in town, who was reportedly also working with sound. This was the same Hans Jenny I had found on my first internet search of "cymatics" years before!

Though Jenny's ideas regarding cymatics weren't of interest to Alexander initially, I found it remarkable that decades later, here he was on his own quest to make sound visible. He was inventing his own ways to see sound—especially in water—while still following in the footsteps of sound-made-visible pioneer Hans Jenny.

I told him about some of my experiences with Dr. Manners, whom he had neither met nor heard of. I shared some of my own work with sound, and how I was continuing the search for ways to use it therapeutically. My mission that day was to introduce him to the Cyma 1000. I was primarily interested in his artistic perspective on how sound images, the building blocks of the universe, become our sacred geometry.

When I showed him my sound device, he seemed very intrigued. Then we discussed how we would connect it to the instruments in his laboratory. He had a lot of equipment, which included frequency generators covering the walls and a transducer on a pedestal in the middle of the room. The transducer was covered with a waterproof tarp, and a black dish filled with water was placed over it. There was a light positioned perfectly above, and a camera focused on the exact spot where he captured the real-time sound images.

We decided to produce some images using the Cyma 1000 right then and there; although, I felt sure there would be a lot of trial and error necessary to get the perfect visual. We continued our conversation while he was preparing for the session.

I learned that we had experienced a similar spiritual journey to India. He had a very impressive statue of Nataraj in his laboratory. It just happened to be an expression of Lord Shiva I have always been drawn to. This was certainly a sign. It made me feel I was in the right place to discover the next part of the information I needed. Knowing about Alexander's spiritual journey made working with the frequencies that reflect sacred chakra energy even more exciting.

We started our process using the frequencies that were part of Dr. Manners' body of work. We chose ones that would have a positive effect on balancing various emotional states.

Since we only had a short amount of time to work, we didn't focus on getting technically perfect images. Yet, they were all incredibly perfect to me: we had created representations of the building blocks of the Divine. Alexander had already been through the process of creating stunning visuals in his own book, so the beauty of the chakra images was of no surprise to him. While we didn't plan any immediate future collaborations, the door was left open. He gave me the cyma glyphs we created to take home with me, which was a generous and precious gift I still treasure.

When I viewed the cymatic images, I contemplated their meaning in regard to the effect on the body when sound is administered. I wanted to understand the interrelationship between the brain, the heart, and how the body systems talked to each other. When I saw these sound-made-visible images in their dynamic state, I observed the miracle of this communication occurring at a high resonance. My quest has always been to discover the most effective way to induce a healing experience facilitated by sound itself.

Later that evening, Alexander and I went to dinner together. During our conversation, I told him that Dr. Manners' work had made me see the importance of the resonant component of sound as a major healing tool. I explained that having the frequencies was only one step though, and finding the most efficient way of delivering them was also extremely important. Alexander was very intrigued by making the Cyma healing sounds visible (the images he was used to seeing were created by one frequency or produced musically). After all, he also had the desire to heal people and was working on that goal with many tools. He expressed support and enthusiasm for my future work.

I felt a deep connection with Alexander. When we sat together and talked, I could see the spiritual creativity in his artistry. In our collaboration with the cymatic images, I definitely felt we were instruments in the expression of the Divine. We came together to watch sound creating form, which is both a scientific and spiritual principle.

On the flight home to the United States, I marveled at how much had happened in twenty-four hours. The experience had been another stepping stone toward the truth. Seeing Alexander's images had provided me with inspiration to continue to pursue my own quest. I realized the incredible treasure I had been given: each frequency was a jewel, a dynamic force of its own.

Chapter Ten

Caretaker of the Codes

I think it is fitting that the first place I saw real-time sound made visible was in John Stuart Reid's laboratory in the United Kingdom, the country where I first learned of cymatics to begin with. I am truly blessed to have met the scientists and innovators whose knowledge has allowed me to see the divine images created by the frequency patterns I championed. The more codes I see made visible, the more I am astounded in their unique manifestations.

In 2008, I became especially interested in the code that is said to open the flow of energy in the meridian pathways in the body. To me, it is one of the most beautiful. Amazingly, it materializes in the shape of a five-pointed star.

This is also indicative of the five elements of Chinese medicine, as well as many other sacred fives that appear so often in our universe. The more investigation I have done, the more I have seen five-pointed-star shapes in many variations of the dynamic states of the codes made visible.

In the United States, the recognition of Cymatherapy is gaining momentum, due in part, to the fascination we have with cymatics. Through this new science, more sounds of the universe are being made visible. Now we can even see the vibratory expressions of the sun and the stars. If we look closely, we can find cymatic images in the ancient symbols of Egypt and India, in the dynamic symmetrical patterns of nature, in temples, in chapels and sacred sites everywhere on earth.

When I first saw an image created by Dr. Manners' frequencies, I viewed it as a building block of the Divine. I recognized it as a pattern similar to those swirls of energy I first witnessed as a child at my church. If we look closely, we can find clues everywhere showing us the interrelationship of science and spirit.

When I look at the list of all the frequencies and their combinations, I sometimes think, "Who could have known all of this? How did they find out? What was the source of this incredible body of work?"

I still remember a conversation I had with Dr. Manners about why he would give it to me. There were many times I thought it was miraculous I even knew about it, and yet, here it was, placed in my hands.

He said, " I am giving it to you because I know you won't change it."

I believe my personal story of my association with Dr. Manners helps to validate the therapy. If Dr. Manners had continued his practice quietly at the Bretforton Clinic and no one had questioned him about his techniques or his successes, then we might never know now what his work could bring to humanity. Through me, hopefully his story will not be lost.

If he were here today, he would assure you that the delivery system is just as important as the frequencies themselves. Listening to a CD will never bring about the same healing experience as having sound administered to your body with the perfect device. It's my heart's desire to share only knowledge that I know to be true. I want to empower others to know what I have learned, so that everyone can take part in their own healing. I hope to live to see science validate all the tenets of sound healing. In the meantime, we must help everyone we can, whenever we can. In this regard, I have been the overseer of miracles.

I still work to understand the information Dr. Manners gave me. Some things he said to me during the first phone call and our initial meetings together were neither fully understood nor fully revealed to me until much later. When I first asked him if he was treating cancer, his answer had been an emphatic "no." What I found out was he had numerous cancer patients, but he wasn't treating them for cancer.

In his cymatic philosophy and his new paradigm of healing, treating the disease wasn't the correct choice. He offered another approach that reduced inflammation and gave support to the body's own immune system to fight the disease. He also insisted that the numerous stresses in each patient's life had to be addressed—all through sound.

As expected, he was getting very positive responses. Patients exhibited increased vitality, the return of a healthy appetite, improved quality of sleep, and a reduction in anxiety. These are all life sustaining signs. The patient's subsequent blood tests, which showed indicators for cancer, revealed numbers that had improved or stabilized instead of reflecting the progressive decline usually associated with the disease. Their years were often extended, due to the numerous ways the body was given help to fight the disease. Everything Dr. Manners chose to do was a step away from or a completely different look at traditional medicine.

In my life in the United States, I am very aware of FDA regulations. As a business owner promoting a device classified as one that relieves stress and pain, it has always been my intention to work within designated guidelines. At the same time, I have always thought I should be able to make sound therapy devices a choice for people who need at-home tools to help them fight the terrible challenges of catastrophic illness. No one should be told there is nothing else that can be done to help them, when there is an alternative that could make a huge difference in the quality and length of their life.

What I choose to do, each time I receive a call from someone who has been given up as a medical lost cause, is to offer Cymatherapy to address the pain, stress, and inflammation associated with a life-threatening disease. With auto-immune diseases so pervasive in our society and the fact that stress has been proven to be one of the chief underlying causes of illness, I believe sound therapy should be available as part of standard treatment to help us prevent the onset of many diseases.

I know part of my journey is to be a caretaker of the healing principles inherent in Cymatherapy, and to do so in a way that will both bless this universe and those who can find healing in the therapy. The cyma glyphs are the visual images of sound healing filled with energy. They are the heavenly flowers of the Goddess, who bestows upon us our health, abundance, and wisdom through her infinite grace.

When I ask myself why I have taken this path, my mind goes back to the life changing phone call when the gentleman first told me about Dr. Manners and sound therapy. It has been a challenging journey all the way through. Whenever the obstacles felt insurmountable and I wanted to abandon the whole venture, I would be reminded by another powerful push forward from the angel who continues to steer me on.

Every day, I work diligently to make sure that Cymatherapy can be an option for everyone. My vision is to see it in every home. I want this incredible form of healing to be accessible whether you have insurance or not. If you are curious about complementary medicine, it is my mission to help. I believe every person should have all the options for healing available to them.

Many times I have witnessed the power of sound and how Cymatherapy works. I know these things first hand.

Chapter Eleven

Patterns of a Vibrating Universe

In 2009, when the United States was being forced to face its financial problems, parts of the Cyma 1000 were becoming obsolete. I was beginning to see that I would have to make huge changes in the manufacturing of the Cyma 1000 in order for the business to survive; I would have to continue developing new sound therapy devices and the techniques for using them. Initially, I thought I could do this while streamlining my first product, but it was becoming increasingly difficult to get parts for manufacturing or repair.

Added to these difficulties, my manufacturing company had made the decision to reorganize their business. Their restructuring dictated they would no longer be interested in employing staff members that made one product for just one customer. My country's tough financial situation was definitely affecting my business, which in turn, affected the development of Cymatherapy.

My perception of how the future would unfold made it clear that I would need to redesign my product altogether. Here were the facts: I had no manufacturing team, no future sales, no engineer, and no parts. The only thing I had left were the frequencies themselves. Reality hit home, and it was a hard state of affairs to cope with. I had to make a decision. My first dream might well soon be over, but I wasn't yet ready for a forced sunset of the Cyma 1000. It felt like (practically overnight) my product, and what used to be wondrous new technology, was no longer the greatest thing ever. I felt cut out and outdated.

The last few units were scheduled to be produced, and I had to consider retiring my device. Not only was it how I made my living, but having as many people in the United States benefit from the therapy as possible was also my dream. I felt a sense of grief over the potential loss of my product, even before it happened. I knew it would be pointless to search for new partners to recreate what I couldn't sustain, but I was incapable of accepting how a product this amazing could no longer be available. Surely anybody who understood the device and its potential for helping people would want to manufacture it.

When I examined other businesses, I saw those involved had no problems creating something new and moving on to the next invention or product. In some cases, people took their creations and sold them to someone else right away. This was not me.

I realized I would have to position myself on a more secure footing—ensuring Cymatherapy production into the future. This, of course, would require a large sum of money. However, there were few choices for me as an entrepreneur. So I made the decision to sell my house and cash in other accounts to generate the capital for embarking upon the next phase of my business.

I spent hours each day lying on the floor in a devastating depression. It felt as if I had lost both my way and the grace of heaven. There was unbearable stress and unrest in my spirit. My nights were filled with fitful sleep and fragmented dreams. Finally, in the midst of it, there was one night that held the most amazing answers for me.

It was part of my spiritual practice, before closing my eyes, to ask for higher knowledge and understanding. More than once, I felt there was a guardian listening to me. Perhaps, there were even more than one who had adopted me for their oversight.

This one night, as I drifted off to sleep, I heard the Cyma frequencies—lots of them. Dozens of images came into view, all linked together. I followed the sound, gliding and floating in the darkness. Then, appearing directly in front of me, there were five interspersed cymatic images. They sparkled and reflected their own light. I felt immersed in the sound imagery.

It was a dream of pure joy.

Astoundingly, there were sound "snowflakes" all around me. It was like looking at crystals through a microscope, but seeing them from the inside out in their purest forms. I felt the vibrating universe. Its infinite beauty was expressed inside of me and out. The first few "flakes" opened and were shown to me in many dimensions. I had never experienced the beauty of images like this before. The lacy patterns played over and over in front of my eyes and traveled through my being. They were dazzling.

Then I awoke abruptly with my heart pounding. My conscious mind was forcing me to try to remember everything I had seen. I was desperate to hold on to the images so that I could discern what their meaning might be. Over the next few days, I felt very disappointed with myself; I had hoped that the dream was a message for me, but I couldn't seem to manifest the answer to my product dilemma or the next step forward.

I returned to the wisdom of the Chinese medicine tenets I had learned to love and trust for my own health. While I was battling my emotional winter, I thought about the cycles of birth and death and tried to believe there was a rebirth in the future of my product.

As in many times in my life, the answer finally came in the form of a vision during meditation. I saw the five elements of Chinese medicine—Wood, Fire, Earth, Metal, and Water—each in swirling globes, filled with layers of knowledge and information. The visuals drew me in. Each one created a pentagonal pathway, revealing a five pointed star shape, further allowing me to see the qualities of the elements. The vision made sense to me on multiple levels. Then the shape of the new device came into view. It would be a plate, of sorts, that could generate healing frequencies.

I realized the codes would enter through the portals of the feet where the energetic pathways begin that speak to the whole body. Then the letters "A," "M," and "I" appeared. A short time later, what they stood for was spoken aloud to me — Acoustic Meridian Intelligence. I trusted the body's *innate intelligence* to utilize the frequencies that would be transported along the *meridian pathways*, with sound we could *hear and feel*. The sounds would be the 750 commutations Dr. Manners had given me to work with — hence the name, the AMI 750.

Shortly after envisioning all of this, my logical mind began to question it. Was this really a possibility? Truth was, I had no choice but to try.

I had a challenging task before me. The consumer needed a user-friendly device. The therapy needed to be accessible to many more people, most of which would not become practicing Cymatherapists. This new instrument had to combine ancient healing principles and Dr. Manners' work, as well as my newly conceived technology. I realized I needed to recreate everything!

As this was a time of rebirth, I felt a new name was in order. Under the umbrella of Cymatherapy International, I chose the legal name of Cymatics Technologies, which would encompass both cymatics and Cymatherapy. In order to compete in the ever-evolving technological industry, I shortened the name to Cyma Technologies (many times, I have just called it "Cyma Tech").

In the meantime, I still hadn't started my work on the new device. Who could I talk to about this? It was difficult because I had no science background. *I* had been given the *vision*.

After speaking with several of my friends, I was finally given a referral to an engineer. Our conversation was pleasant, but he said he had no idea of how to make what I was describing. I met with others then, with similar backgrounds, during this very challenging time. There were several false starts.

With each one, I would begin a long, tedious fact-finding conversation that would always end with the other person telling me what I envisioned didn't make sense, or that it simply couldn't be done. Or, there were those who wanted to put their spin on it. But I was absolutely invested in the vision I had been shown. I was determined to create it.

In the meantime, every day I asked the angels to help me. I spoke my request for a solution to save Cymatherapy each time I went into meditation. It was in my every prayer. Then several months later, the original engineer I had spoken to contacted me. He asked if I had found anyone else to work on my project.

When I told him no, he responded, "Well, I had this dream and I think I know how to make your product."

I was ecstatic.

From spring of 2010, through the three months of summer, we researched my idea of transporting the frequencies through the bottoms of the feet. Using the premise of reflexology and the meridian tenet of Chinese medicine, I believed we could speak to the body via the maps on the bottoms of the feet and the connecting energetic pathways. I felt certain we could access the *human healing potential* by using the frequencies Dr. Manners had given us in this specific way.

We developed the prototype and then contacted a local thermographer for testing. The AMI 750 more than exceeded my expectations. It was matching the efficacy of the Cyma 1000 and continued to quickly reduce—if not eliminate altogether—inflammation in the body! It took a full year and a half to bring the product through trials. The BEMS study had proven the efficacy of the Cyma 1000, and I was feeling confident the new AMI 750 device would meet and exceed these standards—even with the marked differences in their respective designs.

One change was that the Cyma 1000 had magnets in the applicator, which indeed held some benefit. But in consideration for the new design, we recognized that in modern society there are many people with electrically controlled implanted devices. I chose to create a new sound therapy instrument without magnets, safe for all groups of people regardless of their health challenges.

Another new element added to the AMI 750 was the gel pads, used to rest the hands or feet on. I had learned that water-based gel is a great conductor of sound, and it also added an extra level of comfort. At first, I considered using petroleum gel, because it would have been easier to manufacture and less expensive. But in the end, I was determined not to introduce any toxic substances into the design of my new product, regardless of the lower cost or manufacturing ease.

We knew the water-based gel element could potentially make the product more effective. With thermal imaging, we tested (and retested) to find out if the effect of the therapy was greater with or without the water-based gel pads. With them, the new device showed to be 50% more effective in dissipating or eliminating inflammation in the lower extremities than the Cyma 1000 had been. This was expected as these tests were run with the sound administered through the feet. But, during the same tests, results were positive in the chest and upper extremities as well.

Another change was we were now able to address overall disturbances affecting the whole body. The original device with the applicator had been very efficient in addressing specific areas of pain or illness, but with the AMI 750, we were no longer limited to treating just one area. Both sides of the body were being communicated with simultaneously. In cases where clients had pain bilaterally, such as in the knees, we were able to address both areas efficiently and in much less time.

All subjects in the preliminary investigations received thirty-minute sessions of the therapy delivered through the feet. Later we discovered the same efficacy could be obtained when the sound was administered through the hands, which are also portals to the meridian network. For me, this confirmed the ancient teachings about meridian pathways in the body. This made the therapy available even to those who had tragically lost limbs. The miracles of ancient techniques were revealed to me once again.

At the time of our studies, I knew of no research in America that proved meridians existed. In some circles this was considered to be only an esoteric or mystical concept. A few months later, from colleagues on the West Coast, I learned about research that had been published by Joie Jones, a Ph.D. in the radiology science department at the University of California, Irvine.

Jones' experiment consisted of using an 8-hz light flash to stimulate UB67, an acupoint located on the lateral side of the foot. In comparison, he also shone a light into the retina of the eye of a participant. In Traditional Chinese Medicine, UB67 is indicated for the treatment of eye disorders. In the experiment, both responses registered in the visual cortex of the brain, and both were recorded with a functional MRI (or fMRI).

The real surprise being that the rate of response was faster from the stimulation to UB67 through the meridian pathway. Not only did this experiment confirm that meridian pathways exist, but also that communication occurs between the pathways and the brain. The research was so superior in quality that five Nobel prize winners wrote supportive reviews following its publication.

This particular experiment was a great endorsement for the premise of the AMI 750, since its sound commutations were administered through the feet. I was even more excited when I considered the amount of healing potential each of the codes offered. I wasn't just shining a light, I was providing extensive vibrational healing—via information from the frequencies— along these meridian superhighways.

In the fall of 2011, we released the AMI 750 to a small audience of Cymatherapists. This group of practitioners had previously utilized the Cyma 1000 only. My new product, the AMI 750, was a significant departure from this design. It took some convincing for the first few practitioners to accept it. Marketing principles dictate that owners are reluctant to adopt a new product, especially when they are pleased with the original. That being said, the vibrational-medicine field was calling for innovation. I was making decisions with an eye toward the future, and I was hoping the Cymatherapists would join me in my advancement of sound technology.

Admittedly, it is difficult to imagine the body can be healed through the soles of the feet or the palms of the hands, until you experience it for yourself. I always enjoy watching a new client receive specific sound messages, delivered to their body on a cellular level. No matter how technological or mystical their experience might seem, we must remember that the principles of the AMI 750 come from one of the oldest medical systems in the world—Chinese medicine.

The AMI 750 fulfilled my dream of creating a user-friendly, at-home device that makes Cymatherapy potentially available to everyone. In fact, all of the first units that were manufactured were sold. In 2013, it was nominated for the Thomas Edison Award for Innovation in the Fields of Science and Medicine. To this day, I am very inspired to innovate, develop, and manufacture new sound therapy devices—and I've many more on the drawing board.

Once I reached my goal for creating a newly designed device, I knew I wanted to make the contents—the ten channels—evolve as well. Over the years, I have personally utilized many different protocols for both therapy and research. These combinations consist of multiple commutations, or codes, each one with five frequencies. I have personally created *sound recipes* developed with an allopathic or a spiritual approach, as well as a combination of the two. Still, far too often, I was being asked to create protocols for practitioners on a case by case basis.

There was so much information, too many possibilities, and often no consistent response. I knew there could be no definitive research if we continued this way. Once again, I needed more proof before sending therapists out into the community. Consistency in a simplified training for therapists was a necessity.

Dr. Manners spent some years of his life joining his wisdom with the knowledge of others to create the 750 codes that address all parts of the physiology. But if you observed him, not all codes were utilized with every patient. Plus, there was no formal research he could provide me with on any of the protocols.

Over the last fifteen years, I have worked with doctors, nurses, healers, scientists, and researchers to come up with the perfect frequency combinations. They are found in the *Cyma Ten*, which are the fully researched channels in the AMI 750 (that became available in 2016). It took incredible knowledge, skill, and years of study to fine-tune the techniques we use now to speak with the body. And we've only just begun to scratch the surface of the work that has been developed. At Cyma Technologies, we're dedicated to producing the most perfected Cymatherapy protocols, for now and into the future.

People are always asking me about our success stories. Since the release of the *Cyma Ten* channels, we have had stellar responses to our pain protocols. Of all the ways Cymatherapy can help, the most profound examples are associated with reducing or eliminating stress and pain. I also believe our techniques will have a powerful effect on minimizing disease potential overall. Undoubtedly, our world has also become increasingly aware of the pitfalls of drug dependency. Cyma Technologies will continue to research pain protocols to help fight this epidemic.

The world of technology is forging ahead, and I intend to vision my way into it. The devices to deliver the frequencies may change, but I plan to maintain the work of Dr. Manners and his collaborators while at the same time developing it. I will endeavor to bring understanding to these concepts and use them as a foundation to create other sound discoveries. It is important to realize that changing something can mean its evolution, not a destruction of its original essence.

Vibrational sound healing in all its many forms should be preserved and protected into the future. I was introduced to it in meditation via the teachings I received from Baba and in my experiences at many holy places. In my own journey, I have come to understand that sound is part of true healing and is one of the most powerful forces in the universe.

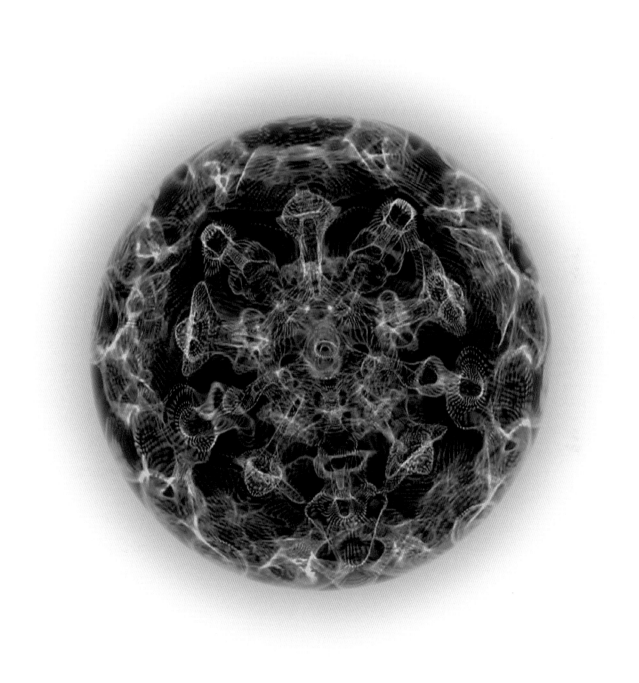

Chapter Twelve

Ancient Ritual, Sacred Sound

For those who have already chosen a spiritual path, sound can be recognized as an amazing natural tool to heal body, mind, and spirit. They are all interconnected. Illness can awaken you to the fact that you have been living with a lack of awareness about your environment and its effects on your whole being.

There are many suggestions for healing based on the elements of the natural world. Our interrelatedness with it is an integral part of our well-being. I'm sure when you've had the experience of visiting a beach or a forest, you recognize how easy it is to move into a more stress-free, harmonious state of being. In the Ayurvedic system, it might be suggested to visit a garden to experience the specific plants that are part of a protocol prescribed for you.

When I consider the science of sound and light, I realize how the concepts have been so brilliantly introduced in the ancient spiritual texts. In the world of scientific development today, there is a great philosophical discussion as to which of these forces came first and what the significance of that might be in regard to physics. According to the unified theory and the new revelations of many scientists and visionaries, sound creates a structure for light to travel through. This is a concept around which spiritualists and researchers can interface.

We are all connected in a multi-dimensional webbing, and within each of us, layers of both physical and subtle components are interwoven. During my early yoga studies, I became aware that asanas, meditation, and chanting could bring our five bodies into balance. Today, we have the more modern-day approach of using therapeutic sound technology to bring coherence to all the layers of being.

The biggest challenge that unravels our divine creation is the issue of stress—and there is no single definition of this word. It can happen to anyone, on many levels and in many ways, which can leave us in disharmony. We cannot reach our optimum resonance of the interrelated five bodies if even one of the aspects of our being is out of sync. Sometimes, if the physical body has been giving us unheeded cues for a while, we will experience disease or lack of coherence in the five bodies. If we miss further calls to action, the disease process can escalate.

In other cases, the physical body can appear to be healthy while other aspects of our being will show the effects of stress. Currently, due to many disturbing events that have happened in our society, there is more discussion about mental and emotional health than ever. Research suggests that some of this mental illness can be caused by an inflammatory process in the physical body. There are also spiritual, emotional, or psychological stresses that can affect the five bodies. If life events cause you to question your beliefs, to have unhealthy perceptions of your relationships, or to experience a lack of purpose—this can result in spiritual and physical pain.

I believe Cymatherapy affects all aspects of the human experience, bringing balance between the physical and the subtle bodies. It is then we are able to live at a higher level of awareness and peacefulness. As we calm stress and put it into perspective we can see our way to a higher state of being.

I continue to seek spiritual guidance to ensure a balanced and harmonious path for Cymatherapy as it moves into the future. But after my first teacher, Swami Muktananda, passed into the heavenly realms, I didn't look for another guru because I didn't believe such a rare gift would be given to me more than once in a lifetime. Then, some twenty-five years later, I was invited to go to a community center for Indian culture in Atlanta to hear Divine Mother Karunamayi speak.

I was very excited to be in the presence of a female spiritual leader. I had read about her many charitable works in the world and knew she was acknowledged as a saint in India. I will never forget how I felt when I first heard her voice. The sweetness of it enveloped me and touched my heart deeply.

The teachings she presented came directly from the Vedic texts. At the end of her discourse, the audience was invited to join her later that weekend at the Hindu temple. I have loved ritual since my childhood—the singing of sacred songs and burning of incense—so it was easy for me to accept this invitation.

Everyone was there to accompany her in chanting the "Lalita Sahashranama," part of the Vedic texts that list the one thousand Sanskrit names of Divine Mother, which extol her many attributes. The entire experience felt so familiar to me. I loved this ritual and its sacred words of intention. I was totally enthralled, astounded that I could be sitting in the presence of an enlightened being—the embodiment of Divine Mother—while together we chanted her one thousand names.

I believe I have been shown two embodiments, the male and female aspects, of two evolved and enlightened beings. I have sacred memories of Baba, and now I have Amma, as she is called. She is Divine Mother Karunamayi, the mother of compassion. I respect her insistence we all do selfless service, and I marvel at the incredible works she has accomplished all over the world.

I love the Vedic teachings she provides, allowing us to be priestesses at the fire ceremonies she conducts in the United States and around the world. At her ashram in the United States, she gives us the opportunity to do the ancient spiritual practices that have always been reserved for other cultures or other times. Now, we can all be a part of the purification process of ourselves and the world in which we live by learning these healing practices.

There have been priestesses in all spiritual traditions since the beginning of time. Women can follow the path, but they can also lead. Divine Mother Karunamayi brings respect to women everywhere. When I visit India, I see the connection of the Vedic teachings through the ages. Meditation comes easily to me there. My experience of the sacred ceremonies is enveloped in memories of the past. I have had the good fortune of loving God for lifetimes.

In spiritual communities, it is being revealed that there are many female gurus on the planet. They are here to anchor the nurturing energy needed by so many at this crucial time in history. I feel Amma's focused attention on helping the world. I believe the wisdom of the past is held in the vibrations of the sacred chants she and many others are now teaching. I see the enlightened soul in her beautiful physical form. She represents for me the possibility of healing the world.

During one of the times she gave darshan in Atlanta, I presented the AMI 750 to her, asking for her blessing on it and on my work in the world. When she gave it, I believed her acknowledgement would take my success to its highest possible vibration.

The task of healing the world is a daunting one. With her, the bigger vision is activated; a path has been created for me to do the highest good. There have been many times during my journey that have been full of doubt and difficulty, with seemingly impossible roads to travel.

Her teachings—her comforting words to me over the years—have helped me to stay the course. During my blessing with Amma, she soothed my soul. When I knelt down before her, her nurturing touch on my forehead was a healing balm. I could hear these words in my heart, "You are on the right track, just keep moving forward."

As I knelt there, she blessed the AMI 750. I knew she wasn't just considering the technological aspect of it; she was also acknowledging my service to humanity. Amma's influence has helped me to understand the timing of each person's healing is an integral part of their spiritual journey. Not everyone will experience the healing they anticipate as quickly as they would like. But many will be immediately awakened to the healing power of sound.

I trust in and count on miracles.

She and many other influential spiritual teachers will certainly be a part of my future evolution of sound technology.

Chapter Thirteen

The Divine Connection

*M*any studies, along with my own personal discoveries, have led me to create what I call the *Soundflower Experience*. In recent years, discovering the healing power of sound has led to the realization that it can be increased exponentially by adding the visual image of it to the therapy. This couldn't have been validated without advances in technology. I'm always looking for the next research project and the newest scientific breakthroughs. Currently, my focus is on projects that show how the sound from the AMI 750 along with the visuals it creates can impact the human energy field and health of the client.

During my search for knowledge, I learned of a new development called *poly-contrast interference photography*. A form of spectroscopy, this system investigates and measures the spectra produced when matter interacts with or emits electromagnetic radiation. This relatively new camera, and the software that accompanies it, allows the practitioner to view what is happening in and around the body in real time. For example, an initial scan is taken of the client by looking into the layers of the energy fields with different filters of the camera. Problem areas that appear to be congested or blocked, physically or energetically, are then identified.

The camera views the client's responses while an outside influence, whether it be a hands-on healer or another form of therapy, attempts to remove the congestion or blockages that could cause disease. Through this technology, it is possible to see if the therapy is having any effect on the energy fields and how quickly.

Of course, I was eager to see what would happen when a client receives Cymatherapy. If my beliefs about the importance of finding and removing imbalances in the energy field were true, I thought I should be able to see the effect of sound during a session recorded by this system. In the last decade, there have been various cameras capable of picking up the vibration of a subtle body or the auric field, but I had not found one that could observe what was happening to the dynamic human form in the moment.

I was also very interested in what the camera would reveal in clients who simply looked at a cyma glyph. Would it be more or less effective than receiving the same healing frequency through the feet? This deduction could not be made using the snap-shot approach provided by other scanning technologies. It would take an observation of the body over time to see the full effect of sound and its visual components.

In some studies, we assessed the usage of the visual images only. The participants simply gazed at specific visual representations (cyma glyphs) of the particular sound being utilized in the study. They all reported benefits, especially in the area of stress relief. In other cases, we applied the sound to the body and showed the images simultaneously, which is more difficult to measure but is also considered highly effective in the area of stress relief and calming the autonomic nervous system (ANS).

My intention is to provide a complete healing experience. For some, it may require all the potential aspects of seeing, hearing, and receiving sound through an application to the body. Clients often have an immediate response to the particular code that is being provided with the AMI 750 without the visual component, whether it be for stress, pain, or other healing possibilities. Some clients gain benefit from simply gazing at or meditating on the corresponding image for the code that addresses their stress or pain. Some clients require a sampling of all techniques.

I had many exciting ideas for utilizing this poly-contrast technology. Fortunately, I learned of a psychologist who was working with it and had taken thousands of scans. She was trained to interpret them and could bring significant expertise to a study using the AMI 750. After preliminary discussions on how to set up the project, we met to begin scanning clients that had reported disturbances in their physical bodies, their subtle bodies, or both. The participants reported suffering from symptoms of stress and pain resulting from work, relationships, or medical issues.

The baseline scans showed *energetic congestion* in the upper torso, head, and throat areas. According to the psychologist, some of the individuals had energy patterns around their heart chakra areas that indicated there were emotional challenges. This was identified in the scan as an *armoring effect*, interpreted as the visualization of the coping mechanism of self-protection. Other candidates showed unhealthy energy patterns around their throats, suggesting the inability to express themselves. Through this system we were able to see visible responses in the scans in both the physical and emotional fields of the client.

Based on their health histories, I chose a specific code and its corresponding images to be utilized in 5 minute sessions on two consecutive days. The subjects were photographed to see the effect of watching a progression of cyma glyphs, created by the same healing frequency, without the transdermal application of the sound to their bodies. Other participants were photographed while hearing the sound and watching the visuals.

The remaining participants had the sound administered through their feet without seeing the glyphs. The assessment tool proved amazing. It was able to show the most minute changes in the energy fields of the clients while we watched. Even the psychologist commented on the immediate visible response of the clients to Cymatherapy. The two-day investigation had netted stunning images. All the final scans showed an improvement in the various health challenges, as we could witness by the change of color and the movement of energy in their bio-fields.

In recent years, I have been in discussions with universities and researchers about creating sound environments that allow participants to be immersed in sound by hearing, seeing its visual, and transdermally applying it to the body. This multilayered experience will certainly manifest in the near future, but in the meantime, I wanted to provide it on a smaller scale for the average person working on their own sound healing. To introduce this concept, I have provided numerous cyma glyphs throughout the book. Information that will give you access to the full *Soundflower Experience* can be found on the "Products and Programs" page at the end of the book.

Without question, the power of the AMI 750 combined with the cyma glyphs had an immediate effect on the participants. I watched as a person's pain disappeared. I saw how the emotions were easily shifted with sound and its visual component. The clients responded to Cymatherapy on all levels.

While watching sound embrace and heal the participants, I have never been more convinced that illness originates in the subtle bodies. I believe energy fields can be repatterned using the frequencies I have researched and continue to work with.

What I call the *Soundflower Experience* is the culmination of many scientific studies and the mystical knowledge that I continue to receive in my spiritual practices. I was moved by the fact that all the participants in the aforementioned study commented on the beauty of the cyma glyphs. In my view, they experienced a kind of coherence—a harmony of the five bodies, related to healing. Our innate awareness recognizes these healing symbols as part of ourselves.

It was no surprise to me that many of the scans showed an increase in the violet light within the participants' energy fields. In sacred studies, this color is associated with the crown chakra, a place of connection to the Divine. This showed me that we are closer than ever to maintaining this connection through sound.

Chapter Fourteen

A Sound Future

I am working diligently to accomplish my original dream of making Cymatherapy available to the masses. People worldwide are using the AMI 750; yet, many more need to know about it. The efficacy of my products point to the possibility of living at the height of wellness. I don't believe we are destined to decline, finishing our lives in a state of illness; there is a much greater health potential we are just beginning to explore.

My personal journey has been that of the *metaphysician*, to whom it was handed the job of confirming spiritual principles through science. The first practitioners who answered the call to learn about Cymatherapy and who have embarked on the training have been instrumental in bringing new awareness. Many of them had no previous traditional medical training, but they chose to believe there were other ways to heal the human body. It has certainly been a courageous journey for both the practitioner and those seeking alternatives, sometimes in the face of the most challenging circumstances. The sound practitioners of today are creating a new healing paradigm and forging a new path.

Sound as a healing modality is being discussed in many different areas where change is needed. I believe the premise of it will soon become widely accepted. This is one of the reasons why I am determined to train people in this career of the future. Every day, I get calls from wellness centers and sports teams looking for new ideas to aid in pain relief and injuries. I hear from teachers in schools who are starting to believe sound can help children focus. More doctors are adopting sound techniques as complementary medicine. Many potential private owners contact Cyma Technologies because they have made a decision to create their own pathways back to health.

Dr. Manners couldn't explain to me exactly how cymatic therapy worked, but from years of experience in his own practice, he knew that it did. He drew upon the knowledge of many, to come to his own conclusions. It became his truth, after long years of research and the experience of caring for his patients. There is still much to know, but without a doubt, I have witnessed people heal with sound therapy. For years I have waited for science to provide the proof of what I have already personally experienced. I have kept the faith and will continue to do so.

Dr. Manners foresaw a day when each of us would be identified by our own individual vibrational *biosignature*. He believed that in case you were injured, or in an accident, there would be a specific configuration of frequencies on file that could be used to regenerate your physical form through sound. Your biosignature would be preserved for future replication. He referred to this as the harmonic factor in the cells, or the "H Factor."

In the future, I believe it will be possible to regenerate our bodies during a restful night of sleep. In our homes, we will be surrounded by the healing vibrations we need. We will wake up repaired and in full resonance.

We already know that sound can balance the brainwaves. Through this, we may learn to use a higher percentage of the brain, helping us to evolve into a species of higher consciousness. I envision an entrainment factor, meaning that when more of these elevated beings are on the planet, the rest will rise to the same level of awareness. A golden age upon the earth will then be possible.

What must be done now, is the continued research of the frequencies and the development of the unlimited commutations—along with the best devices to deliver them. We must all work in every aspect of life to address the needs of a world suffering from unprecedented pain. With therapeutic sound, it is possible to help humanity with many of the stresses we face. The frequencies generated by the AMI 750 produce a deep state of relaxation in minutes. The healing sound can reduce anxiety, erase fearful thoughts, and help to alleviate pain.

When I observe a person on the AMI 750, I see a whirlwind of energy encompassing their subtle bodies, from the feet upward. Many people close their eyes during the session. When their attention turns inward, I witness how sound brings cohesion. As areas of stagnation clear and the bodies move into harmony, there is a free flow of energy. The cells are listening.

In public presentations, we invite the participants to experience the AMI 750, all at the same time. When this happens, the participants report there is an energy that builds in many layers, which they have felt awaken in their own bodies. Our collective healing experiences draw us together. It makes it possible to see the amazing power of sound, which is a major tool for bringing the whole person and the whole planet back into harmony.

Through the work of my colleagues, I have been able to see the imprint of sound on the cells of the human form. It is thrilling to know we can activate the temple of the body with sacred sound and the images it creates. I have been blessed beyond measure to know scientists, healers, and artists with vision. They, too, believe that true healing can be discovered and available for us all. We can continue to apply what has been learned to live a healthier life, to bring ourselves and the world back to a centered sense of well-being.

...The body can remember its original song.

Postscript

In 2016, when I was scheduled to return to the United Kingdom to further my research with healing frequencies and cymatic images, I felt an overwhelming urge to go to Bretforton and see Dr. Manners' old clinic. Even though I knew his office had closed in early 2005, I wasn't sure what had happened to the facility itself. The last letter from his wife reported he had developed dementia, which saddened me greatly. The opportunity to connect with him on any level was now gone. I just needed to see the clinic one more time.

I asked the taxi driver to park some distance away, so I could quietly relive my memories while walking the narrow streets of the small village. When I arrived at the clinic, I walked up to the front door and knocked. After a pause, when no one answered, I soon realized that the estate had become a private residence. I was filled with waves of emotion as I looked at the building that was the location of my first visit with Dr. Manners. We had shared so many miracles.

As I walked away, from a distance I saw a young family arrive with a baby carriage. Another new life-story was beginning in the same place where my own story with Dr. Manners had come to a close. I walked into the neighboring shops and restaurants, and I spoke to people who still remembered their "old country doctor." Little did they know, right in their midst, he had been providing for them some of the most profound keys for healing the body. He had given much to his colleagues, patients, and friends.

Looking back, the fact I received that first phone call telling me about Dr. Manners had been nothing short of a miracle. My heart is filled with peace because I know I responded with full force to the angelic vision that propelled me forward on that first day, and I am extremely grateful I can continue to play a part in making Cymatherapy available to the world.

While the visit to Bretforton brought closure, it was also bittersweet. I drove to the nearby lake, close to the old church I had visited almost daily during my years of study with Dr. Manners. I had spent many prayerful hours there when I had been overcome with doubt. In this town full of memories, people appeared to be living their lives as if nothing had changed.

Whereas I live in a technological world that moves at a pace faster than any of us could have ever imagined. I sometimes wish for simpler times and easier days.

However, it's hard to rest when I know there are many who are suffering. It is given to me and many other visionaries to know how best to carry sound healing forward. I do feel the pressure, and I know the clock is ticking; yet, I am also filled with anticipation about the enormous possibilities of the future.

— The sound flowers have opened a doorway.

ACKNOWLEDGEMENTS

There was so much love given to me all along the way…

From my Angels and Guides

my family and friends

the visionaries and pioneers who join me in pressing forward

my spiritual brothers and sisters who help me open the doors

the practitioners and staff at the Bretforton Clinic

the courageous people who put their faith in sound therapy

the doctors who have opened their minds and hearts

the professional people who use these healing principles in their lives every day

those who helped create and continue to bring forth ISTA

those in the veterinarian field who cherish our animal kingdom

the professional athletes and sports medicine practitioners

the celebrities who have given their endorsement both publicly and privately

and all the Certified Cymatherapy Practitioners

…I am happy to share OUR story.

My team of miracle workers has been immense. Here are some of their names:

Marcia Christman, Phillip Christman, John & Annaliese Reid, Jeff Volk, John Beaulieu, Elizabeth Bauer, Margaret & Steve Ruby, Jim Kegley, Dr. Anthony Fleming, Dr. Keith Cooper, Dr. David Lee, Don Simmons, Lois Grant, Dr. Maoshing Ni, William Meyer, Dr. Rhett Bergeron, Dr. Susan Kolb, Steven Halpern, Dr. Susan Russell, Jonathan & Andi Goldman, Dr. Heather Mack, Professor James Oliverio, Pat Lynch-Barrett, Dr. Robert Gilbert, Jonn & Anne Serrie, David Crosby, Monique Myrick, Reverend Tiffany Barsotti, Dr. Paul Mills, Harry Oldfield, Thornton Streeter, Astera Manis, Marie Dahle, John Enge, Kate Holland, and Anthony Bove.

GLOSSARY

activated: when spiritual practices cause the *shakti* associated with kundalini yoga to begin to move upward from the base of the spine

adivasi: a collective term for indigenous people of mainland south Asia; *Sanskrit* word specifically coined for the original inhabitants of any area; 8.6% of India's population

AMI 750: a therapeutic acoustic sound device invented by Mandara Cromwell; AMI (Acoustic Meridian Intelligence) device emits sounds that travel the meridian pathways of the body; 750 refers to the frequencies included in the body of work developed by *Dr. Peter Guy Manners*

ANS: Autonomic nervous system: a control system that acts unconsciously and regulates body functions such as heart rate, digestion, and respiratory rate; it has two divisions, which are the sympathetic nervous system and the parasympathetic nervous system

ashram: a place where a person or a specific group of people go to live apart from society; a spiritual community that is instructed by a *guru* in meditation or spiritual matters and studies

Ayurveda: a *Sanskrit* word that translates as "wisdom of life" or the knowledge of longevity; a health system developed by the sages of India, views health as much more than just the absence of disease; thought to be more than 3,000 years old

Bailey, Alice: a writer of more than 24 books on Theosophical subjects; one of the first writers to use the phrase "New Age;" she wrote her books under the tutelage of a Tibetan teacher

Blake, William: an English poet who was recognized as being a seminal figure of the Romantic Age who valued imagination over reason; from childhood, spoke of having angelic visions

Brahmin priests: Hindu priests and teachers who protect sacred learning across the generations

brahmacharya: a yogic practice meant to encourage participants to conserve their sexual energy in favor of using it for spiritual advancement

chi: life force energy—a feeling of aliveness according to *Chinese medicine*; natural energy pattern of circulation in the body, similar to *prana* in the Ayurvedic system

Chinese medicine: based on 5,000 year old tradition; includes herbal medicine, acupuncture, massage, and dietary therapy

commutations: the process of combining energies, or frequencies, for a specific purpose or response in the body

cyma: ancient Greek word meaning "wave" or "swell"

Cyma Ten: the ten channels found on the AMI 750 device, containing frequency patterns developed by Dr. Peter Guy Manners; researched protocols by Mandara Cromwell for the evolution of sound therapy

cymatics: the study of wave phenomenon; the science of sound made visible

darshan: spiritual discussion, meeting, or discourse with a *guru*

Divine Mother Karunamayi: a female *guru* who is revered across the world as an embodiment of Divine Mother due to the compassion she showers liberally on everyone she meets; a voice for humanity, she is a global leader for peace and has initiated numerous charities to aid with education, medical care, clean water, and eradicating poverty

EST training: a technique created by Werner Erhard in 1971, which brought to the forefront ideas of personal transformation, personal responsibility, and accountability—it became a sign of the times in the 1970s

The Farmer's Almanac: a publication originally founded in 1792; a reference book that contains weather forecasts, tide tables, planetary charts, astronomical data, and helpful hints on many topics; it is updated on a yearly basis

Ganesha: the elephant-headed God that is one of the best known and loved deities in the Hindu pantheon of gods; the god of wisdom and learning, remover of obstacles, and a sign of auspiciousness; one of the most recognized spiritual symbols outside of India.

guru: an enlightened teacher in eastern religions who takes the student or aspirant from spiritual darkness to light

I Ching: ancient Chinese divination tool, also known as the Book of Changes; one of the oldest Chinese classics

ISTA: the International Sound Therapy Association; a 501c3 nonprofit organization founded in 2005 by Mandara Cromwell, dedicated to increasing the awareness of the power of sounds in the environment, provides education through classes, workshops, and conferences; it promotes the use of therapeutic sound to support health and collects research on the use of sound modalities from ancient traditions as well as modern technology

Jenny, Dr. Hans: a Swiss physician and natural scientist who published the book *Cymatics: The Study of Wave Phenomenon;* developed work on the effects of sound vibration on fluid, powder, and liquid paste; coined the term *"cymatics"*

jyotisha: the science of light that involves sacred gemstones

karma: the sum of a person's actions in this and previous states of existence, bringing upon one's self inevitable results that can be good or bad

khus oil: also known as vetiver oil, offers a heavy earthy fragrance reminiscent of patchouli, but with a touch of lemon; believed to have a grounding, calming and stabilizing effect

kriyas: in *Siddha yoga*, spontaneous postures, breath, and sound that work together for a natural unfoldment and spiritual transformation of body, mind, and spirit

"Lalita Sahashranam": a Vedic Sanskrit chant that reveals the 1000 sacred names of Divine Mother, describing her attributes, transcendental beauty, and universal powers

Lauterwasser, Alexander: a German photographer and researcher who created work using the science of *cymatics* (sound-made-visible); in 2002, he published *Water Sound Images* showcasing the imagery of water surfaces set in motion by sound

mala: a string of beads used in meditation practice; can be made of many materials such as authentic gemstones, sandalwood, or rudraksha seeds; believed to help the practitioner focus the mind

Manners, Dr. Peter Guy: a pioneer in sound therapy who collated the work of German scientists relating to *cymatics* research; he developed cymatic therapy using acoustic sound waves to improve health conditions

mantra: a word or sound repeated to aid concentration in meditation; a Vedic hymn, a statement, or a slogan repeated frequently to provide motivation and to focus the mind; words that express basic beliefs

marma points: an important element of Ayurvedic healing power, developed in India centuries ago; energy points that are said to facilitate deeper levels of healing

medical intuitive: an alternative medicine practitioner who uses intuition to find the causes of an emotional or physical condition

Nataraj: Lord of the Dance; a form of Lord Shiva which is an extraordinary example of the rich and diverse culture in India; a clear image of the activity of God experiencing the rhythm and harmony of life

Goddess Parvati: wife of Lord Shiva who depicts the ideal example of family love and unity, seen holding red and blue lotuses in her hands; known for bringing peace to the cosmos

poly-contrast interference photography: an energy-field video imaging process using experimental technology which reveals patterns of light not visible to the naked eye; a method or process driven by an intricate system of calculations and formulas that provides real time moving images of an energy field

prana: all cosmic energies that permeate the universe on all levels; vital life force flowing through energy pathways in the body

pranayama: the formal practice of controlling the breath for specific purpose

prasad: a devotional offering made to God, typically a food—later shared amongst devotees

protocols: groupings of codes joined together within a channel, used for specific purposes or healing responses as part of a planned healing routine; sounds that are transmitted by the *AMI 750* device

reflexology: an ancient healing technique originating with early Egyptians; it includes the application of pressure to specific points and areas of the feet, hands, or face—the points correspond to different body parts and organ systems—the result of which is to stimulate the body's own healing potential

Reid, John Stuart: an English acoustics researcher who studied the physics of sound; a respected authority in the field of *cymatics*; inventor of the CymaScope, a device to make sound visible

reincarnation: the rebirth of the soul into a new body; a transmigration of the soul

Rife, Raymond Royal: an American inventor in the 1930s; one of his devices, the Rife machine, was a frequency generator that could kill or disable diseased cells; his theories centered around finding specific frequencies to kill specific pathogens

rudrakshas: beads that are sought after for mystical and medicinal properties—the varieties, colors, shapes, and numbers of cuts on the beads determine the value; the word is derived from "rudra" (another name for Shiva) and "aksha" (eyes)

Sacred fives: the number five is the number of manifestation; within the five elements are all the components necessary for creative manifestation; other sacred fives include the five elements of *Chinese medicine*, the five platonic solids, the five senses, the five pillars of Islam, the five books of the Torah, and the five subtle bodies of the Vedas; the five pointed star holds significance in many traditions

Sanskrit: an ancient, classic, literary language of India, used in Hindu scriptures and classical Indian epic poems; the language from which many northern Indian languages are derived— developed in regard to the natural progression of sounds created by the human voice

shakti: a female principle of divine energy, especially when personified as the Supreme Deity; the activating power of consciousness

Shiva Purana: one of eighteen Sanskrit texts in Hinduism that centers around Shiva and the *Goddess Parvati*; suggests step-by-step yoga practices

Shiva temple: a place of worship dedicated to Lord Shiva, recognized as Lord of Yoga, destroyer of ignorance

Siddha yoga: a spiritual path founded by Swami Muktananda to honor the lineage of Siddhas who are initiated by descent of divine power; seekers must be awakened by a *guru*; once active, this inner power is said to support the seeker's steady effort to attain self-realization

sound healing: to stimulate healing with singing bowls, crystal bowls, or therapeutic sound devices, such as the *AMI 750*; sound therapy that uses the human voice, or objects that resonate, to cause the client to have a deeply relaxing experience

spectroscopy: the study of the interaction between matter and electromagnetic radiation, originated through the study of visible light dispersed according to its wavelength by a prism

subtle body: one of a series of layers of energy; the physical body consists of energy that vibrates slowly (allowing us to see it), while subtle bodies connect to the physical form via energy points, or chakras—this directs energy into the physical body via the meridian system

Swami Muktananda: a leader of the *Siddha yoga* movement, who traveled the U.S. in the 1970s and '80s; his reputation as a meditation master spread throughout the world, and people came by the hundreds to sit in the presence of a living master who could transmit the direct experience of inner joy and wisdom to his devotees

Unified theory: a model in particle physics where several forces or interactions are merged into one force

The Vedas: the most ancient spiritual texts composed in *Sanskrit*, containing hymns, philosophy, and guidance on how to live and perform sacred rituals; believed to have been revealed to seers in India originally handed in an oral tradition, the first writings appeared in 1500-1000 BCE; the oldest texts known to civilization; the spiritual literature of the ancient Indian culture

Vedic astrology: an ancient Indian divine science which studies planetary movements and their effects on the twelve signs of the zodiac; utilizes *jyotisha*

Volk, Jeff: an American poet, producer, and publisher; popularized the science of *cymatics*, the study that shows how matter can be influenced by vibration

yagna mandap: a temple, porch, or structure where sacred rituals are performed, usually with openings in the roof for the release of smoke during fire ceremonies

BIOGRAPHY

Mandara Cromwell,

D.C.M. (Doctorate of Cymatic Medicine),

is an American woman entrepreneur and

inventor, who is also the CEO and President

of Cyma Technologies. This company,

built on spiritual principles, manufactures

her own inventions—the AMI Acoustic

Meridian Intelligence devices. The AMI 750,

an advanced sound technology device, was

nominated for the Thomas Edison Award for

Innovation in the Fields of Science and Medicine in 2013.

In 2002, she coined the term "Cymatherapy" and used it to refer to *wave therapy* based on the work of a group of German and British scientists, which included Dr. Peter Guy Manners, with whom she studied. Since that time, she has taken his work to new heights with the development of the delivery systems innovated in the AMI devices and the fully researched protocols found within them.

Long years of study and research inspired Ms. Cromwell to create Cyma Technologies, in order to preserve the integrity of these specific healing frequency patterns. In 2016, Ms. Cromwell released the most fully researched frequency healing protocols in the United States, as part of the programs found in her devices, and named them the "Cyma Ten."

In addition to her profit making company, she is the founder and board chair of ISTA, the International Sound Therapy Association. Since 2006, ISTA has been serving the field by producing the annual Cymatic Conference, which draws together new voices in sound science. The organization has provided community outreach in numerous cities and continues to offer ongoing classes in therapeutic sound education with both ancient instruments and cutting edge technology. She currently co-chairs the organization's national initiative, the Pain Free Living Campaign. This project was designed to educate the general public and provide them with drug-free, noninvasive sound solutions for pain relief.

In 2017, Ms. Cromwell produced the conference entitled "Cymatics: The Art and Science of Making Sound Visible," during which she revealed never before seen cymatic images of healing frequencies. The program also premiered a short film entitled "dance divine," which she co-produced with other artists, utilizing dance, yoga, and healing-sound images.

Ms. Cromwell holds a B.A. in Art History, which led her to studies in Eastern philosophy and a journey to India, where she first encountered sacred sound. She travels the world lecturing on sound as the medicine of the future. She was invited by the Indian Cultural Ministry in 2013 to share her presentation "The Art of Sacred Sound" at the Sacred Art Symposium in New Delhi. A frequent guest on radio and television programs, she speaks about the healing power of sound and how to access it through ancient techniques and her own innovations.

With her many endeavors, she still finds the greatest joy in her three grandchildren and hopes to enrich their lives with her wisdom and spiritual experiences.

Products and Programs

For information on Acoustic Meridian Intelligence devices (AMI devices), and training programs for careers of the future in Cymatherapy, visit www.cymatechnologies.com.

AMI devices are manufactured for use by professional healthcare practitioners and private owners. Cyma Technologies offers **exclusive certification programs** for those desiring to become Certified Cymatherapy™ Practitioners (CCPs), as well as certification programs for AMI Facial Rejuvenation Therapists. **Online courses** are available, along with live workshops, conferences, intensives, and retreats (which are held throughout the world).

Cyma Technologies also provides **private owner programs** to empower individuals who choose Cymatherapy as part of their wellness program.

Now that you have read "Soundflower," we invite you to discover a new state of the art video compilation of "cyma glyphs" -some of which you enjoyed in this book. This collection of stunning visuals comprises *The Soundflower Experience.*

Gazing into the sound-made-visible images creates a deeply relaxing, visual delight which brings an almost instant relief from stress. *The Soundflower Experience* can be an introduction for meditation or enjoyed as a tool for health and spiritual growth.

Visit our website at www.CymaTechnologies.com to purchase *The Soundflower Experience* for your continued and unlimited viewing pleasure.

Tell Your Friends to Join Us in the Discovery of the Cymatic Universe!

Soundflower by Mandara Cromwell

More People Are Talking About *Soundflower*!

Flossie Park, sound healer, Director of Yoga Teacher Trainings, Encinitas, CA:

"*Soundflower* invokes an excitement about the world of possibilities in the realms of understanding sound and its effect on all of creation, as well as our own well-being. Mandara's passion, vision and determination about the potential of sound is clearly a life purpose. Showing up for her journey, trusting the process as it unfolded, the pieces of the puzzle came together to create a new picture of how science and spirituality are blended. This is the answer many of us have been looking for. This is the next step in our conscious evolution.

"Thank you, Mandara, for never wavering in your inner knowing. You inspire us to remain steadfast regardless of deterrents along the way. As for the future of sound healing, you are truly a visionary and your book, *Soundflower*, is pointing the way. My deepest gratitude!"

Forrest Smith, M.D.:

"*Soundflower* relates an incredible journey of a remarkable woman, divinely led to create a unique medical device using audible sound frequencies for healing. The book describes her life path from early childhood religious experiences through encounters with physicians and scientists working with sound. Her biography lends amazing insights into the principles of sound and how it can modulate health at the cellular level. The principles of bioenergy, whether light, ultrasound, or magnetic resonance are currently being used by hospitals and doctors. Ms. Cromwell is extending that usage into audible sound frequencies for healing. As an integrative medical doctor who has practiced conventional allopathic medicine alongside homeopathic medicine, I welcome the AMI 750 as an impressive therapeutic modality. I feel confident that the medicine of the future is bioenergy."

Tracee Dunblazier, spiritual empath, shaman, and author of the national award-winning book series *The Demon Slayer's Handbook*:

"Mandara Cromwell tells her activation story and growing relationship with the science of *sound healing* with a compassionate voice and indelible commitment to forge the path for the masses. This book offers not only important information on the work and study of Cymatherapy, but also brings to life for the reader that being spiritual means channeling the wisdom into your daily life choices. No matter what—you can."

J. Winston, meditation teacher:

"What a fascinating story! It is a testament to listening to your instincts and following your heart, while pursuing your dream. I look forward to more of the world catching up with Mandara and others' belief and vision for sound healing."

K. Watkins, engineer, Yoga student :

"Reading about Mandara's life and her discovery of Cymatherapy was inspirational. Her story is proof that intention, meditation and being open to possibilities leads to amazing things."

C. Echelson, marketing executive with personal endorsement:

"I have used Cymatherapy for the past five years and can speak to the amazing benefits that it has on my mind, body and soul—from helping me to manage stress, to eliminating the pain from a pinched nerve in my neck. I was thrilled to read Mandara Cromwell's *Soundflower* to learn about the history of Cymatherapy and how it came to the United States. Her story is both beautiful and courageous—one that makes me appreciate Cymatherapy even more."

R. Parker, counselor:

"The realms of healing that surround us are reaching out through Mandara Cromwell, to bring the power of sound into a form that can heal human pain and suffering. She has remained loyal and fierce in her commitment to the higher realms to bring sound therapy to a world in need. To read her story is inspiring and teaches us to listen to and trust our own holy leadings."

Marielle Croft, astrologer:

"*Soundflower* is a well written, fascinating story. The flower images throughout the book are rich with resonance. I was moved by the intimate sharing of Mandara's personal dreams and visions. Both her life and her book are full of magical encounters."

Joy Rodino, Esq., certified Cymatherapy practitioner and author of *Fifty-two Words My Husband Taught Me—Love, Inspiration and the Constitution*:

"This extraordinary book beautifully chronicles the sacred journey of a modern visionary as she listens to her heart and follows her guidance to manifest the power of sound as a healing modality in our time. Mandara's inner light fills the pages of this inspirational introduction to Cymatherapy and its unlimited potential for healing the world."

Steven Halpern, Grammy-nominated recording artist, sound healer:

"Modern science is continuing to confirm what ancient sound healing and mystical traditions have understood for thousands of years. The vibrations we perceive as sound are the fundamental building blocks of our three dimensional physical world. We can learn to harness the healing power of sound in many ways, as we explore the efficacy of using it as a therapeutic modality. Mandara Cromwell's new book, *Soundflower*, is a welcome addition to the field and should help introduce the concept to a much wider audience.

"In my own evolution as a composer, recording artist and sound healer, I first met Dr. Manners and learned of the cymatic research in 1977 at the Festival of

Mind, Body And Spirit in London and immediately understood that it provided 'sound evidence' that needed to be part of the holistic and complementary medicine revolution. I am delighted that *Soundflower* will continue and expand this revolution."

Howard Beckman, author of *Mantras, Yantras and Fabulous Gems*:

"*Soundflower* is the story of one woman's journey on the path to learn about the ancient healing art of sound. Having been graced with both the researched and inner knowledge of the science by a master, she set out to bring it to the world. Marrying the spiritual essence of the sacred discipline with modern science, she has created the way to bring sound healing to our world, in a way that all people can take advantage of. Mandara Cromwell is sure to become one of the world's most important wayshowers of sacred sound healing, called *cymatics*, of the 21st century."

Jonn Serrie, composer and producer, and Anne Serrie:

"Mandara Cromwell shares a spiritual journey that will have a lasting impact on the science of sound and healing. Her pioneering research in the field of Cymatics has led to a new paradigm in spiritual awareness and the healing power of sound in its many expressions. *Soundflower* informs and inspires. We highly recommend it!"

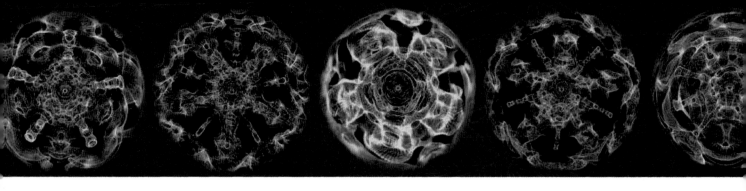

Soundflower Notes

_____

_____

_____

_____

_____

_____

_____

_____

_____

_____

_____

_____

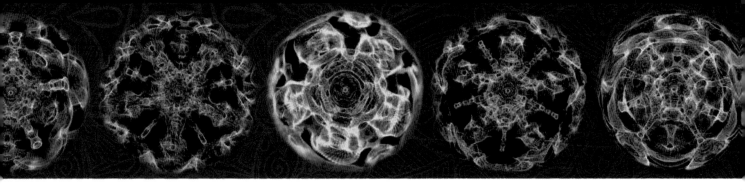

Soundflower Notes

_____

_____

_____

_____

_____

_____

_____

_____

_____

_____

_____

_____

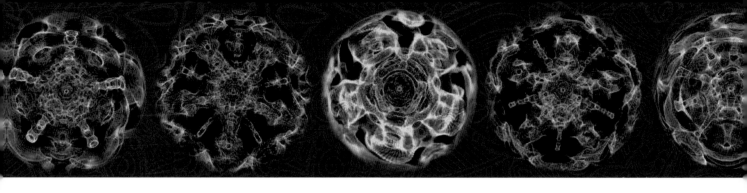

Soundflower Notes

_____

_____

_____

_____

_____

_____

_____

_____

_____

_____

_____

_____

_____